BUILDING DIVINE

intimacy

BUILDING DIVINE

intimacy

HOW TO BECOME A DAILY
DISCIPLE
OF THE LIVING GOD

TONILEE ADAMSON & BOBBYE BROOKS

Building Divine Intimacy:
How to Become a Daily Disciple of the Living God

ISBN 10: 0-9788726-4-9
ISBN 13: 978-0-9788726-4-9

Tonilee Adamson and Bobbye Brooks
P.O. Box 131780
Carlsbad, CA 92009

Published by HonorNet
P.O. Box 910
Sapulpa, OK 74067

CONTENTS

INTRODUCTION

WHEN WE FIRST BEGAN THINKING ABOUT writing a book, the initial thought was: "Let's help people learn *how...*" How can we truly know the Lord personally? How can we understand the Bible? Does God really speak to us? How can we be sure we are hearing His voice? So many questions, but did we have the answers? If there are real-life answers to these real-life questions, then wouldn't the lives of Christians be changed forever? YES! This book was written with an intense desire and prayer to help you find answers that will change your life forever. The answers are available, and this book is a step to get you started in finding them.

Although we (Tonilee and Bobbye) have very different backgrounds and life experiences, we became friends when we began praying together. We realized almost instantly that praying together brought a vulnerability and humility before each other and before the Lord. The more we prayed, the more we began to sense the Lord working. The more we prayed, the more we experienced the love of God as He answered those prayers. The more we prayed, the more we changed...and even our prayers began to change. We then began reading the same Bible version in conjunction with a daily reading plan. As we were reading the same scriptures each day, the Lord began to speak and confirm His Word to us. The combination of the Word and prayer began to change our lives...individually and together. It was as though the Lord was invading our thoughts, desires, and activities. The black-and-white areas of life began to turn into living color.

THE MORE WE PRAYED, THE MORE WE CHANGED... AND EVEN OUR PRAYERS BEGAN TO CHANGE.

While being involved in women's ministry, we realized that many people in the church do not understand this kind of relationship with the Lord. How could we help others sense His leading, hear His voice, be comforted by His Word, and answer His call? These things were exceptions and not the rule to the committed, professing believer. The Lord came to be a part of every aspect of our lives. He has placed His Holy Spirit in us and given us everything we need for life and godliness. He has given us His Word and prayers that reach the very throne of God because of His mercy. Yet many Christians battle fear, insecurity, and guilt every day. We learned firsthand that God has so much more for each of us—things that are founded on His love, God's unconditional and never-ending love.

So, within a couple of years, we started writing Bible studies because we wanted to teach others how to read and apply the Word of God to their lives. The key is to do it...*daily,* so we designed a Bible study to serve as a daily devotional in the Word. Each day has scriptures, questions, applications, and prayer. We knew from our own lives that this recipe was the key to unlocking a spiritual change in whoever committed to doing it. So we used the material in a women's Bible study group…and it worked! The Bible study grew and women's lives began to change. The Word of God applied to their lives combined with fellowship, accountability, and prayer led to absolute, phenomenal changes. Knowing God and His power is a life-changing experience.

We have since been committed to teach others how to have a daily walk with the living God. And it is a daily walk, a process of building divine intimacy. For us, this walk never ends, and the journey is never boring. We have written this book to testify to this divine intimacy by using our very own life experiences, backed by the Word of God, to help others find His love, joy, and peace as well as the abundant life that Jesus promised. Heaven starts here, as Jesus left His Spirit in all of us who believe, and believers today are the only agents who can represent His love, hope, and wholeness for which He died.

Our prayer for you is that you make this daily walk a priority in your life. This book will get you started walking and it will help you understand the steps you will take. Intimacy with the living God will fill you with an irresistible love that will change your life and most likely, those around you too.

Chapter 1

Divine Intimacy

What's in It for You?

I (Bobbye) live in Southern California, but I was born and raised in Tennessee. My mom and one of my sisters are still living back there. I have another sister who lives in Georgia, and a sister in Texas, so you could say we cover the Southern belt of this country. As I was talking to them recently, I was thinking how much I really would like them to live closer to me because I miss seeing them. We are never too far away from talking to the people we love, even if we do not live in the same town, but although I talk to them on the phone quite often and we send each other e-mails all the time, I miss being with my family.

If you have people you haven't seen for awhile, do you ever stop and think what it used to be like to be with them? We often just miss being in their presence because there is nothing that can take the place of that intimate, personal, face-to-face type of communication.

How many of us ever long for that kind of close relationship with the One who loves us unconditionally—our heavenly Father? Yet He created us for divine intimacy.

Does it surprise you to hear that the living God, Creator of heaven and earth, wants to know you in a close, personal way? Nothing in this world can replace having that kind of intimacy with Him. It is crucial to our happiness and well-being in life. We can pray to God, we can read the Word of God, and we can go to church (which we should do regularly). But if there's no intimacy with the Lord, then we're missing the purpose of our salvation, which is to have a relationship with God right now, not just when we get to heaven.

IF THERE'S NO INTIMACY WITH THE LORD, THEN WE'RE MISSING THE PURPOSE OF OUR SALVATION...

When you go to church or you gather together in a church setting or a Bible study, where is your heart? What are your reasons for going? Do you go because it's what you're supposed to do? How many Christians really go to church and expect to have an experience with God? Better yet, how many leave church and expect to have an experience with God?

Why do we go through the motions of a Christian life if there's no evidence of a Christian life—if there's no joy in our hearts and no fire within us, despite our circumstances?

It is only in that place of intimacy with God, that extraordinary place of being in His presence—not in being married or remarried, not in having children, not in a job or in decorating a house or buying a new car or in anything else—that's going to bring you real joy. We have written this book to let you know that you can have this amazingly intimate and personal experience with the Lord every day.

Can you think back to a time when you truly knew you were in God's presence? Maybe it's been quite a while. Do you ever miss or long for that face-to-face contact with the Lord? Do you really remember His voice, His touch, the one-on-one type of communication you had with Him? Maybe you've never experienced being in His presence, and you don't have a clue and you're wondering, *How do I really experience the presence of God in my life? How can I find that intimacy with the Lord?*

If you want more of God, to truly know Him better, and you want to find out how to enter into that special place of intimacy with Him, keep reading, because we have designed this book to help you to answer those questions and to build the kind of divine relationship with the Lord that will cause your life to radically change.

Being face-to-face with God means we are talking. It's personal. It's intimate. Nothing is hidden, and believe me, there is nothing hidden with God. He already knows everything about us anyway. (See Psalm 139.) I (Bobbye) don't think it's a coincidence that the Hebrew word for *presence*, which is *paniym*, means "face."[1] I believe that God purposely chose that word to let us know that we can be with Him face-to-face, in His presence, in that place of reverence, speaking to Him as we speak to a friend.

> IF YOU WANT MORE OF GOD, TO TRULY KNOW HIM BETTER... KEEP READING.

Jesus himself verified that in the New Testament when He said that He no longer calls us servants, but He calls us friends (John 15:15.) He gives us the clearest proof of that friendship by opening to us His mind and making known to us His plans[2] (1 Corinthians 2:16) because we have His Spirit.

"God is Spirit..." (John 4:24). So how do we have a relationship with Someone whom we cannot see, hear, or feel physically? How do we as human beings find a place of intimacy with a Spirit? We talk about it sometimes as if we know it should happen because we are Christians, but do we truly know what it means to us personally?

Throughout this book, we will be exploring the fundamental components that are essential to finding intimacy with God. Our emphasis will be on practicing them daily—going beyond just learning about God—because change can only occur in your life when you apply (or practice) what you have learned.

You may be thinking, *But if we are Christians, then God is always with us so why do we need more?* That's the point; we do need more. If God is always with us (and He is), then why do we sometimes wonder what is missing in our lives?

There's a reason you are reading this book, and if I (Tonilee) were venturing to guess the possible reasons, I'd say it has to do with your feeling that something is missing in your life. You may know that you know the Lord, but it may not always seem to come together and you're not always sure that He's with you. Or maybe you've had glimpses of really being in His presence and you just want to go back to it, but you don't know how you can get back there.

Perhaps there's a void in your life. I believe we're all born with that empty place inside of us that only God can fill. So if you are not experiencing God's presence regularly, you are not complete. Before Bobbye and I show you how to find that place of intimacy with the Lord in His presence, you need to understand that it is the only way you can be completely fulfilled as a person, as a Christian, as a child of God.

I BELIEVE WE'RE ALL BORN WITH THAT EMPTY PLACE INSIDE OF US THAT ONLY GOD CAN FILL.

No matter where you are in life, no matter what is going on, no matter where your walk is with Christ, the answer lies with the Lord. There is no answer that you are looking for that He doesn't have. When you practice seeking His presence, He is more than willing to unfold everything He has for you and lead you into an exciting and victorious Christlike life.

In this next section, we're going to expand on living that kind of life by looking at the extraordinary life Moses led because of his relationship with God. One of the reasons we chose his story is that it shows what's in it for you when seeking the presence of the Lord is your number-one priority.

FACE-TO-FACE ENCOUNTERS

The first time Moses came into God's presence, God spoke to him from a burning bush on the back side of the desert. At that time God called him to deliver the children of Israel from Egyptian bondage; He wanted Moses to lead them to their destiny of the Promised Land. (See Exodus 3.)

You probably know the story, how God brought ten plagues on Egypt until finally Pharaoh gave in and set the Hebrew people free. That very day they started out on a forty-year-long journey to the fulfillment of God's promise to bring them to a land flowing with milk and honey. Eventually Moses and the Israelites came to Mount Sinai and set up camp there while Moses went up to the top of the mountain to seek the presence of the Lord and receive further instructions.

During that time God told Moses to build a tabernacle as a physical place to come into His presence. This passage from Exodus shows us how God planned to visit His people there.

Moses took his tent and pitched it outside the camp, far from the camp, and called it the tabernacle of meeting. And it came to pass that everyone who sought the LORD went out to the tabernacle of meeting which was outside the camp. So it was, whenever Moses went out to the tabernacle, that all the people rose, and each man stood at his tent door and watched Moses until he had gone into the tabernacle. And it came to pass, when Moses entered the tabernacle, that the pillar of cloud descended and stood at the door of the tabernacle, and the LORD talked with Moses. All the people

saw the pillar of cloud standing at the tabernacle door, and all
the people rose and worshiped, each man in his tent door. So the
LORD spoke to Moses face to face, as a man speaks to his friend.
And he would return to the camp, but his servant Joshua the son
of Nun, a young man, did not depart from the tabernacle.

—Exodus 33:7-11

This tabernacle is not the tabernacle that Moses would later build
according to God's specifications to hold the Holy of Holies and the
Ark of the Covenant. Yet it was a place where God's presence would
descend in the form of a cloud to speak with His prophet Moses.

God could not be seen in physical form lest the people would die,

SO OFTEN WE
WANT TO SEE
SOME KIND
OF TANGIBLE
MANIFESTATION
OF GOD.

so He revealed His presence to them in the
form of a cloud. The first time we see this is
when He led the Israelites through the desert
in the form of a cloud by day and a pillar of
fire by night (Exodus 13:21). Now we see His
presence revealed to them in the tabernacle
Moses built.

The people would come out of their
tents and from a distance they would watch
the Lord descend on the tabernacle in the
thick cloud (Exodus 19:9). When they saw
that cloud descend, they knew that Moses

was with God, having a conversation, talking, speaking with Him,
face-to-face.

Can you imagine what that must have been like? It's hard to
conceive, and yet we have God's Holy Spirit within us (if we are
born again) in the same way that God came down into that tent. But
so often we want to see some kind of tangible manifestation of God,
like that cloud, come down in our lives.

The Israelites could see the manifestation of God's presence in
the form of that cloud, and they would stand and watch reverently

and even worship Him, but they would not talk to Him face-to-face as Moses did. They tried it once and were so terrified that they begged Moses to continue to be the one to enter into God's presence and tell them what He said (Exodus 19:16; 20:19).

You may be wondering why Moses set the tent up way outside the camp. It represents to us the importance of getting away from distractions to be alone with God, but it was also "to signify to [the Israelites] that they had rendered themselves unworthy of [God's presence], and that, unless peace was made, [His presence] would return to them no more."[3] What had the children of Israel done to jeopardize being in God's presence? They had turned away from Him and worshipped an idol instead.

THE CAMP REPRESENTS TO US THE IMPORTANCE OF GETTING AWAY FROM DISTRACTIONS TO BE ALONE WITH GOD.

Moses had been up on Mount Sinai receiving the Ten Commandments from God, and God and Moses were totally together on that mountaintop for forty days. (See Exodus 24:12-18.) What an extraordinary experience that must have been for Moses. Yet in the meantime the Israelites, who were down at the bottom of the mountain, got tired of waiting for his return and, as the story goes, they decided to build a golden calf to worship instead of worshiping God. They had never wanted to experience being in God's presence regularly for themselves, so it probably wasn't hard for them to decide to worship an idol.

Aaron [Moses' brother] told them, "Take off the gold rings from the ears of your wives and sons and daughters and bring them to me." They all did it; they removed the gold rings from their ears and brought them to Aaron. He took the gold from their hands and cast it in the form of a calf, shaping it with an engraving tool. The people responded with enthusiasm: "These are your gods, O Israel, who brought you up from Egypt!"
—Exodus 32:2-4 MSG

The children of Israel actually threw their ornaments into the fire to melt into gold, which they used to make the golden calf. Those ornaments represent anything in our lives that we put before God—those distractions in our lives that often lead us down the wrong path. When that happens, those things can become idols to us, that in a sense we are worshiping, and they can cause us a lot of problems.

THAT ACT OF DOUBT AND UNBELIEF CAUSED THEM A HEAP OF TROUBLE.

The Israelites began to worship the idol of the golden calf instead of God, and that act of doubt and unbelief caused them a heap of trouble.

GETTING BACK ON COURSE

At some point in the midst of God speaking to Moses on the mountaintop, God stopped and told him to get back down that mountain and deal with his people. When Moses reached the camp and saw what they had done, he threw the stone tablets to the ground which broke them in pieces; then he took that golden calf, burned it in fire, ground it up, and made the Israelites drink it (Exodus 32:19-20). Obviously Moses was quite upset!

Needless to say, God was quite upset too, and Exodus 33 opens with a type of aftermath of this situation. God was angry, Moses was angry, and the people were feeling remorseful. Moses decided that he had to go back up to the top of Mount Sinai to seek atonement from God for the people's sin, and God and Moses talked about what was going to happen to the Israelites.

Let's read about it first and then we are going to step back and look at what God is really saying to us through these verses.

Then the LORD said to Moses, "Depart and go up from here, you and the people whom you have brought out of the land of

*Egypt, to the land of which I swore to Abraham, Isaac, and Jacob,
saying, 'To your descendants I will give it.'"*

—Exodus 33:1

In other words, God was telling them to get back on course, to
head back down the road because they had a destiny and He was still
going to fulfill His promise to them—but there would be a change
from the original plan.

*"I will send My Angel before you, and I will drive out the
Canaanite and the Amorite and the Hittite and the Perizzite
and the Hivite and the Jebusite."*

—Exodus 33:2

The "ites" were the Gentile nations that lived in the Promised
Land. God was telling Moses that He was going to drive them all out
of there because He was giving that land to His people.

Notice what else God said: "I am not going with you, but I am
going to send My Angel to go before you." In other words, "I am
going to substitute for Myself and just send My Angel." This next
verse tells us why the sudden change occurred.

*"Go up to a land flowing with milk and honey; for I will not go
up in your midst, lest I consume you on the way, for you are a
stiff-necked people."*

—Exodus 33:3

God was saying here, "I am not going because I am so angry with
you, I'm afraid I'd destroy you along the way." Sometimes we need
to realize that God can get upset with us—*Without faith it is impos-
sible to please* [God]... (Hebrews 11:6)—but He is also merciful, and
His character is a character of faithfulness and promise and love and
steadfastness. He had a promise He had given His people, and He

told Moses that He would keep the covenant He made with Abraham about giving the Israelites the land of Canaan.

Fortunately we are under the new covenant, made when Jesus died on the cross, which changed our relationship with God for the better (we will talk about that later on), but under the old covenant He denied the Israelites what they'd been blessed with so far—His presence going with them—and left them under the hand of Moses and the protection of a guardian angel.[4] They had endangered their relationship with God, and they were not happy about it.

> *When the people heard this bad news* [that God's presence wasn't going with them], *they mourned, and no one put on his ornaments. For the* LORD *had said to Moses, "Say to the children of Israel, 'You are a stiff-necked people. I could come up into your midst in one moment and consume you. Now therefore, take off your ornaments, that I may know what to do to you.'" So the children of Israel stripped themselves of their ornaments by Mount Horeb.*
>
> —Exodus 33:4-6

In this passage God told Moses to tell the people to take off their ornaments or don't put them on. Matthew Henry in his Bible commentary explained that "God bade them lay aside their ornaments, and they did so, both to show, in general, their deep mourning, and, in particular, to take a holy revenge upon themselves for giving their ear-rings to make the golden calf of."[5]

We saw earlier that the children of Israel threw some of their ornaments into the fire to melt into gold, and Aaron used that gold to make the idol of the golden calf. Those ornaments symbolize anything that we value more than we do the Lord. When that happens, God will tell us "Strip them off," because they can become an idol to us and keep us out of His presence.

I (Bobbye) had to learn how to seek the Lord in my life. I always wanted God to come alongside me. I loved all the verses about answered prayer, about prosperity and success and God's blessings. I loved reading them and quoting them back to the Lord, but it didn't really equip me for the trials that would come into my life, and I would say to the Lord, "Why are You doing this to me? I am not doing this to me." But really I was the cause because I hadn't stripped off all the ornaments and given myself totally to God. That is the purpose of trials.

God doesn't cause bad things to happen to us, but He can use them to get the ornaments off of us. My ornaments were title, paycheck, power, success, and credentials among others, and God was saying to me, "Strip off those ornaments, Bobbye." You may be fighting God to keep from stripping off the ornaments in your life. Just remember that God's presence is with you. If you have received His Son Jesus into your heart and you have His Holy Spirit living inside of you (which we'll discuss later), then God is right there with you. The question is, are you with Him?

GOD DOESN'T CAUSE BAD THINGS TO HAPPEN TO US, BUT HE CAN USE THEM TO GET THE ORNAMENTS OFF OF US.

We don't always want to come to the Lord like that because we know that place of worship, that place of vulnerability, that place of humility means going through some kind of experience like the Israelites went through when Moses made them drink the burned up, ground up golden calf idol. It was terrible, but that's how some of us are. It takes that kind of situation to get our attention on the Lord.

We don't always want to come to God in humility and worship and say, "Okay Lord, I give up; help me," yet we desperately need to reach that place where we can say that and tell Him, "Lord, I am not going to take one more step until You and I get right."

DIALOGUING WITH GOD

Moses was in a trial, wouldn't you agree? He had over a million people there who had just lost their minds and worshipped a false god, and somehow he had to figure out how to get them to the Promised Land. Now he had just found out that God would not be going with them, but he wouldn't accept that, and he began to discuss it with the Lord. Verse 12 gives us a clue about the conversation they were having.

> Moses said to the LORD, "See, You say to me, 'Bring up this people.' But You have not let me know whom You will send with me. Yet You have said, 'I know you by name, and you have also found grace in My sight.' Now therefore, I pray, if I have found grace in Your sight, show me now Your way, that I may know You and that I may find grace in Your sight. And consider that this nation is Your people."
>
> —Exodus 33:12-13

Moses was not only talking to God here, but he was now beginning to reason with Him. Basically Moses was repeating back to the Lord what the Lord had said to him, which is one of the reasons we need to be in the Word of God. We're going to cover the Word more in a later chapter, but there is tremendous power when we take the Word and say it back to God.

Can you see the dialogue going on between Moses and God? Moses was actually putting the responsibility of the situation back on the Lord. "Wait a minute, God. You are checking out on me and not going with us after all? That was not the deal we worked out. Do you know who You are sending with me?" Moses, speaking face-to-face in God's presence, was saying that God had only told him, in general terms, that He was going to send His angel. Yet the Lord had told Moses that He knew Moses' name and that Moses had found grace in His sight.

Does God know you by name? Yes, He does, and He hears you when you talk to Him because that is one of His promises to us. (See Jeremiah 33:3; 1 John 5:14-15.) When we know that He hears us in that intimate, face-to-face relationship we have with Him, we can start talking to Him about what is going on in our lives. You may be thinking, *This was Moses.* No, this is every single one of us who believes.

The point is that when we find ourselves in trials, we need to be in the presence of God, talking to the Lord as Moses did. But if we haven't been practicing God's presence in our lives, we're not going to know what He has been telling us all along, and we won't be able to go back to Him and say things like, "Lord, I don't understand what is going on; this is not what You told me," as Moses said.

Moses knew what God had told him and he reminded God, "... *this nation is Your people*" (Exodus 33:13), thus putting the responsibility of the Israelites back on the Lord. I (Bobbye) love that because it caused God to change His plan and say, *"My Presence will go with you, and I will give you rest"* (v.14).

[GOD] HEARS YOU WHEN YOU TALK TO HIM BECAUSE THAT IS ONE OF HIS PROMISES TO US.

If that were me (Bobbye) and God had just changed His plan for me, I might be saying, "Oh, thank You, Lord, for going with us after all! I didn't want that Angel to go," even though *Angel* is capitalized in several Bible translations and some biblical scholars say that this angel could have been the preincarnate Jesus himself. Yet Moses responded, *"If Your Presence does not go with us, do not bring us up from here"* (v. 15). It was as if Moses were saying, "If You don't go with us, I am not going to do this and we are not going."

Do you ever talk that way with the Lord? It is hard to have this kind of dialogue with God unless we learn how to be in His presence on a daily basis.

We've been laying a foundation here for the kind of fulfilling, life-changing experience that practicing the presence of God can be for you. Moses went from a stuttering sheepherder on the back side of the desert to a strong man of God who spoke boldly to Pharaoh and led over a million people to the Promised Land. You too can rise into the plan God has destined you to fulfill when you know how to truly practice His presence every day.

YOU CAN RISE INTO THE PLAN GOD HAS FOR YOU WHEN YOU KNOW HOW TO TRULY PRACTICE HIS PRESENCE EVERY DAY.

How can your life change by being in God's presence? How can you be made whole and complete? Why should you care?

These are valid questions. In fact, one of the questions that Tonilee and I try to ask ourselves before we teach a Bible class is pretty simple, "What's in it for them? When you hear a teaching or you come to church or you come to a Bible class or conference, if you are honest, you are probably wondering, "How will I be blessed by this teaching?"

Three truths from the story of Moses in Exodus 33:14, 16 show you what's in it for you when you practice the presence of God for yourself.

1. MY PRESENCE WILL GO WITH YOU

God is saying to us in this passage the same thing He said to Moses, "You are in My presence; My presence is with you; I am going to go with you." You may be thinking, *How does that pertain to me? Where is God going with me?*

So often we hear from people who are at a crossroads in their Christian walk. If you are walking with the Lord every day, you are going to find these places in your life too, where you are wondering, *Do I go over here or do I go over there? Do I wait or do I move forward?* Then there are times when we get stuck in the rut of wondering,

Should I have ever come this direction in the first place? We can get all twisted in our thinking, but the good news is that God's presence can lead us, guide us, and direct us.

There is a plan and a purpose for every single one of us in the Lord, and the ultimate goal is the same one the Israelites had—the Promised Land. Of course, ours is not the same physical Promised Land that God gave to the Israelites, but so often we are unclear about a situation and pray, *Lord, I am just not sure which way to go,* and we stop there.

How many times do we say to the Lord, "I am not taking one more step until I know You are going with me"? Have you ever said that to God? That's the importance of being face-to-face with the Lord—you know how to hear from Him, how to be led by Him, and you don't want to take one step without Him. If you come to Him with a sincere heart, then He can lead you in the right direction.

I (Bobbye) was thinking about that as we were preparing to write this book, and my dog came to my mind. I have an adorable basset hound named Buddy who runs my house; there's no doubt about it. I'm sure it's my fault because he is spoiled rotten, but there is absolutely nothing Buddy likes to do more, outside of eating, than going for a walk.

YOU DON'T
WANT TO TAKE
ONE STEP
WITHOUT
HIM.

In my house we cannot say, "Let's go for a walk." We have to spell out the word *walk*—W-A-L-K—because that dog will hear us and he'll be right at our heels, waiting to go outside. I am usually the one who walks Buddy every day, but on occasion, something will come up where I can't go with him.

Recently I had to go somewhere right when Buddy was due for his evening stroll, so I asked my husband, Tom, "Would you take Buddy out for me?" I was still in the house, but I had to leave in a few minutes, so Tom grabbed the leash and we both said *walk* out loud, and Buddy was so happy. As usual, he was at the door in a second. I put the leash on him, and they walked out toward the gate that goes into our front yard.

In a moment I left my house and started to run out to my car as Tom and Buddy went through the gate. They walked to the left and I went to the right to get into my car, but I realized I forgot something so I ran back into the house. When I turned around to come back out the door, I saw that Buddy was still at the gate. Tom had the leash, but as I opened the gate, Tom and Buddy were standing there, and Tom said to me, "He won't go without you."

Buddy is just a dog, and it is probably mostly habit, but he refused to go on his walk—what he loves to do more than anything else—without me. I admit there was a part of me that felt, "Aw, he can't go without me," and it kind of blessed me. That may seem silly in reality, but think of it in relation to God. How much must it bless God's heart when we refuse to go anywhere or do anything without Him?

WE CAN FEEL HIS PRESENCE AND IT IS WONDERFUL, BUT WE NEED TO *LIVE* IN HIS PRESENCE EVERY DAY.

Aren't you touched when someone says, "I just can't do this without you"? Wouldn't that bless our heavenly Father's heart if we came to Him and said, "Lord, I am not going without You; I just want to be with You"? How do we get in God's presence to even know which way to go? Do you remember what Moses did? He set up his tent outside the camp. Moses would come into the camp, but when he wanted to be in God's presence, he would go back out to that tent.

We can talk about God's presence and at times we can feel His presence, and it is wonderful, but we need to *live* in His presence every day. We need to have those moments when we set up our tent outside the camp—away from distractions—and spend time alone with the Lord.

Do you have a place in your life that you go to spend time with God? Do you set aside time to be face-to-face with Him? Do you know how to bless your heavenly Father's heart? Do you know how to come to Him and share whatever the situation is that's in your heart and say, "Lord, I am just not sure about this; I'm confused," and get down on your knees in reverence and prayer? We will be covering these concerns in-depth throughout this book, but first we want to make one point clear right at the beginning.

SPIRITUALLY SPEAKING, WE ARE THE TENT, THE TEMPLE OF GOD, AS HIS HOLY SPIRIT IS LIVING INSIDE OF US.

You saw earlier that the children of Israel would bow down in the doorways of their own tents, and they would worship God. The sad thing about that is, Moses was the only one there who would come into God's presence. Thank God that we don't need to sit on the outskirts. We can come to the tent and enter into the presence of God ourselves.

Spiritually speaking, we are the tent or the tabernacle, the temple of God, as His Holy Spirit is living inside of us when we are born again (1 Corinthians 6:19), but we need to make the effort to practice His presence. We need to make it our lifestyle to seek the Lord; to ask Him for wisdom, guidance, and instruction; and tell Him, "Go with me, Father. I am not taking one step without You."

2. I WILL GIVE YOU REST

You may be wondering why you need God's presence every day. Do you need rest? Do you need peace? You are not going to find it in the world. Even the Bible warns us that this world isn't going to get better. Jeremiah 6:14 talks about those who shout *"Peace! Peace!"* but there is no peace. Our peace will ultimately come when Jesus returns to take us home. (See 1 Thessalonians 4:16-17.)

In reality, the life we live here on this earth is not one that will be filled with the kind of rest and peace the world offers. Jesus told us where our peace comes from, *"...in Me you may have peace. In the world you will have tribulation; but be of good cheer, I have overcome the world"* (John 16:33), and He promised us rest (Matthew 11:28). Does that rest mean we don't have to do anything? We can just kick back and relax? I (Bobbye) don't believe so because of what Moses had to go through to lead the Israelites into the Promised Land.

JESUS TOLD US WHERE OUR PEACE COMES FROM. "...IN ME YOU MAY HAVE PEACE."

Was Moses resting? I doubt it, but he had a supernatural, spiritual touch of peace and rest from God. Despite what was going on, he had God's promise to him, *"My Presence will go with you, and I will give you rest"* (Exodus 33:14). In other words, "I am going to make it seem at times as if you are still and calm on the inside, regardless of what's happening on the outside."

Have you ever been in the midst of a storm and yet you felt like you were in the eye of it? Hurricanes are horrendous on the outskirts, but the eye of the hurricane is very calm and peaceful. That's what it feels like when we are with God and we are in His presence. It's as if we've entered the "God zone."

I (Bobbye) accepted the Lord when I was nine years old, and I know that I knew Jesus as my Savior that whole time in my life, but I was extremely ambitious. Many people are constantly strung out on stress and anxiety whether we want to be or not. Just look at the pace of everything we do. There is no rest in this world, but I had no concept of that. I didn't even think about it because it's an issue of pride.

People today, including Christians, become proud of how much we can accomplish, how much we can achieve, how fast we can keep going in life. I was like that too. I never even gave peace and rest a second thought, and by the time I was in my early thirties, I began to have terrible stomach problems, migraine headaches, lower back pain, and problems sleeping.

I had a very successful career in health care. I was in executive management by the time I was twenty-eight. In addition to working at a job that required a seventy-mile drive one way every day, I was studying to get my executive MBA. I was so far beyond myself that I had no idea that there was something I didn't have—God's presence. I never even thought about it, yet I went to church, I prayed every day, I read my Bible, and I talked to God in the car. (I had lots of time in the car!)

This is the scenario for so many of us in our Christian walk. We read the Bible, pray, go to church (which are all important), and we have that component in our lives, but we don't understand the reality and importance of practicing God's presence too.

ARE YOU IN THAT PLACE WITH THE LORD OF BEING AT REST DESPITE EVERYTHING ELSE THAT'S GOING ON AROUND YOU?

It would be a little while later on before I realized what it meant to truly worship the Lord, practice His presence, and enter into that place of rest. It took some very serious trials in my life to bring me there. What about you? Are you in that place with the Lord of being at rest despite everything else that's going on around you?

You may be in some kind of trial right now and are not sure how it is going or where it is going to end up. Let me encourage you with the fact that Moses was in trials as well, but look at what happened to him as God used him. Wherever you are today, and whatever trial you may be facing, God promises you, "I am going with you, and I am going to give you rest despite whatever is happening in your life."

3. WE SHALL BE SEPARATE

Why do we need God's presence so badly? The reason is that we are supposed to be separate from the people who are in the world. Are you truly living separately? Now we're not saying the Christians over here, and the non-Christians over there. That's not what we are called to be. We are called to spread the message of the Gospel, to be lights in a dark world. But unless we are in God's presence, unless He is going with us, unless we are finding peace and rest in our lives through Him, we are going to be like the world.

I (Bobbye) remember when I got to that point of surrender—when I went from being very sick physically, emotionally, and mentally to being made whole. Because I was living without the presence of God, I wasn't complete and made whole until I found and set up my tent and took off my ornaments and came and sought the Lord regularly. When I did, I was able to help others as well.

Until we get right with God, until we deal with Him regarding the things that we need to get right in ourselves, we are not going to be of much service to anybody else. It's when we're willing to say,

UNTIL WE GET RIGHT WITH GOD... WE ARE NOT GOING TO BE OF MUCH SERVICE TO ANYBODY ELSE.

"Lord, do whatever You need to do in me so I can be set apart from the world and be totally Yours," that we can make a real difference on the face of the earth.

God called the nation of Israel to be His nation, His holy nation, His people, and to be set apart. That was so important because the children of Israel were getting ready to go into the Promised Land where all the Gentile nations were pagan and living a terrible lifestyle. We actually live in a world today that is pagan. The lifestyles around us are atrocious.

But individually, because we have this incredible privilege of being face-to-face with Holy God, we can be set apart from the world and its pagan ways.

Christians are sanctified. We have been redeemed. But if our lives do not show that—if we don't bear witness to it—we are not complete; we are not whole. We are not what God intended us to be in His plan for us. Fulfilling His plan depends on being face-to-face with Him.

We want you to live in the power and presence of the Lord every day, but more importantly, God wants to be with you personally. Hard to believe? He wants to be with each of us and has given us everything we need to make that possible. Yet we can't talk about God's presence and how to have a close, personal relationship with Him and look at all the blessings that come from that relationship if we're not sure that we have His presence living in us.

So before we look at what the Scripture says you need to practice in order to experience divine intimacy with God, we're going to share with you where living in His presence starts—in your heart.

BUILDING BLOCKS
■■■■■■■■■

■ Question 1: What does the presence of God mean to you? Describe in your own words how to really practice His presence.

■ Question 2: Why did God want Moses to build a tabernacle?

■ Question 3: Read Exodus 33:7-11 to answer these questions.
  a. In what way did God make His presence known to the people in the tabernacle?

b. Can you describe a way that God has made His presence known to you?

■ Question 4: Read Exodus 32:2-4 to answer these questions.

   a. The children of Israel threw their ornaments into the fire to make the golden calf to worship. What do those ornaments represent in our lives today?

   b. Why do you think it was so easy for the children of Israel to worship a false god made out of gold?

■ Question 5: How did practicing God's presence change Moses' life? How can it change yours?

■ Question 6: Read Exodus 33:14,16 to answer this question.

   a. Write down in your own words the three truths from this passage that show you what's in it for you when you practice the presence of God.

Chapter 2

BELIEVE AND RECEIVE

The Foundation to Everything

M Y (BOBBYE) MOM GOES TO A CONSERVATIVE, denominational church—one that I was raised in and have visited many times. She called me recently and was asking me how things were going with our ministry, but I could tell that there was another reason for her phone call. After a few moments, she became really excited and said, "I've got to tell you what's happening in our church."

"Great, Mom, what's happening?" She told me, "People are getting saved!" That wasn't what I expected to hear, and I told her rather matter-of-factly, "Well, that's good, Mom, people are supposed to get saved in church."

"No, you don't understand, Bobbye," she said. "People who have been in church their whole lives are getting saved!" Then she began to tell me about one particular lady.

This woman walked down the aisle during the altar call, went up to the pastor, and when she had finished talking to him, she turned around and professed in front of the whole church that she had just accepted Jesus as her Lord and Savior—and the whole church was shocked because she'd been going there for years!

She told the congregation, "I walked down this aisle when I was seven years old. I prayed the sinner's prayer. I was baptized in water, grew up, got married, had a family, and raised my children in church. I lived a good life and didn't really do anything bad, but for years I've known something was missing. I've had this knowing, or this *something* within me that just didn't seem right, and now I know what it was. I never knew how to truly walk with the Lord and live with the Lord and really know He was in my heart."

Here's the most stunning thing about this story: the woman is seventy years old! That means she went from the age of seven to seventy without knowing how to have a close, personal relationship with her heavenly Father. Evidently all those years she didn't know that she could come into the presence of God or how to get there.

YOU CANNOT LIVE IN THE PRESENCE OF THE LORD UNTIL YOU ACCEPT JESUS.

The truth is, you cannot live in the presence of the Lord *until* you accept Jesus and He is living in your heart by the power of the Holy Spirit.

Our desire in this chapter is to show that the foundation of everything in the Christian life is Jesus, so we're going to begin with our relationship to Him. Then we will lay a scriptural foundation of who the Holy Spirit is and how He affects you daily so that you will be able to practice the presence of the Lord.

The gospel of John in the New Testament starts by discussing Jesus, who is the Word made flesh (John 1:14), coming as the Light into the world. John was a beloved disciple of the Lord, and in his writing he told us how to become God's children.

But as many as received Him [Jesus], *to them He gave the right to become children of God, to those who believe in His name.*
— John 1:12

Is it really that simple? Yes, it is. *Believe* means to entrust one's spiritual well-being; to have faith in Christ. *Receive* means to take, to get hold of. In our modern world, it seems as if God is in, but believing, receiving, and living for God is not. If that is true, then many people are living a dual life. They are filled with good feelings about God in faith, but they are in control of their own destiny and operate apart from Him.

You may not realize it, but a person can believe in Jesus and say the right words in a prayer of salvation without believing in their heart that Jesus has truly saved them and without wanting Him to be their Lord. You see, there is *Savior Jesus* and there is *Lord Jesus*. Many Christians want *Savior Jesus*, but very few want *Lord Jesus* because *Lord Jesus* requires a walk of life that means giving up control.

A PERSON CAN BELIEVE IN JESUS...SAY THE PRAYER OF SALVATION... WITHOUT WANTING HIM TO BE THEIR LORD.

It took sixty-three years for the woman at my mom's church to realize this. We don't want that to be your story. That's the reason we've written this book—to help you to find out what walking with the Lord and being in His presence are all about so you won't live your life for years wondering what's missing.

We tend to toss around the heart frivolously nowadays, making statements like "Oh, my heart's just with the Lord; I gave my heart to the Lord, and I love Him and want to be with Him," without really knowing what that involves. The issue of the heart is more complicated and much deeper than we may realize because the heart needs first of all to be in a place of repentance.

John the Baptist was a contemporary of Jesus, but John's ministry started before Jesus'. John was the forerunner to prepare the way for the Messiah, and he had one main point when preaching—*repent!* The purpose of John's ministry was to prepare the hearts of the people to realize that they were sinners who needed a Savior.

We cannot accept Christ as our Savior unless we're willing to repent of our sins, but beyond that, practicing the presence of God involves an attitude of repentance in our hearts every day, continually. We can say, "Lord, forgive me of my sins," or we can say, "Lord, forgive me for that thought I just had," or "Lord, forgive me for that word that just came out of my mouth," or "Lord, forgive me for being unkind to that person," or anything else we've done that we know is wrong. We don't need to wait until we get to church to confess our sins or wait until the next day or the next week.

We can be in a continual state of repentance before the Lord in our hearts by telling Him about what we've done and asking for His forgiveness right away.

IF WE REALLY SAW WHO WE WERE BEFORE THE LORD, WE'D DO NOTHING BUT REPENT.

The fact is, if we really saw who we were before the Lord, we'd do nothing but repent. But it's by His grace that we are forgiven, and it's in the place in our hearts where we've made Him *Lord Jesus* that we're able to walk with the Lord and in His ways.

Walking in that kind of life is possible when our hearts are open before the Lord to change. We're going to talk more about changing our minds later on, but that's really what repentance is all about—and it begins with changing our hearts and letting Jesus in and surrendering our lives to Him.

You can see the resistance to that way of life in someone whose attitude is, "It's not my fault," or "I've done nothing wrong. I'm not repenting of anything." There's one big problem with this kind of attitude—when we do that, it keeps God out.

Can you see now why being in God's presence starts with the attitude of your heart? It's not, "Oh, Lord, forgive me of my sins," and going on with your day. First, it is asking Him, "Lord, quicken my heart if I've done something wrong. If there's anything I'm doing that's keeping me from You, please convict me of it in my heart [He doesn't ever condemn us]. I know that I keep failing in this area, but I'm going to keep asking for forgiveness because Your mercy covers everything, and my sins are not going to stand in the way of my relationship with You." Then it's repenting of whatever He shows you.

You can also ask for His help before you commit a sin. I (Tonilee) got really good at allowing the Lord to tell me I did something wrong after I did it. But it took awhile for me to get to the point of allowing Him to help me to know if I'm in a place where I could possibly sin *before* I did it.

YOU CAN ALSO ASK FOR HIS HELP BEFORE YOU COMMIT A SIN.

I encourage you to learn to ask the Lord to show you the potential for sin in a situation before it happens, because you can repent afterward, but very likely you're still going to have to bear the consequences of either the words that you said or the attitude that you had or the action you took. If you will ask Him beforehand, you will avoid quenching (restraining or suppressing) the Spirit of God working in your life, and you will be able to come to Him about other issues as well.

So coming into God's presence begins with accepting Jesus as your Lord and Savior and having a repentant heart—in other words, it starts with becoming born again.

BORN OF THE SPIRIT

The third chapter of John talks about a man named Nicodemus who was a nationally known and respected religious leader. He was not only a Pharisee but a member of the Sanhedrin, the council of the seventy most outstanding Jews. He was a righteous, church-going religious leader who knew the law. This rabbi knew the Scriptures in the Old Testament. But he saw what Jesus was doing and recognized that He was no ordinary man. He had to be sent from God.

One night he came to Jesus to get some answers and said, *"Rabbi, we know that You are a teacher come from God; for no one can do these signs that You do unless God is with him"* (v. 2). What was Nicodemus saying?

How many people sit in church week after week and say, "I'm a Christian, I know God, I pray, and I read His Word"? I am not talking about the god in another religion here. I'm talking about people who say, "I know Jesus," the one true God. Basically, that's what Nicodemus was saying, but Jesus saw straight through him and He replied, *"Most assuredly, I say to you, unless one is born again, he cannot see the kingdom of God"* (v. 3).

Nicodemus was puzzled by His statement and said, *"How can a man be born when he is old? Can he enter a second time into his mother's womb and be born?"* (v. 4). Notice that this is a physical response to a spiritual statement. This is someone who heard Jesus' statement in the earthly (or natural) realm rather than in the spiritual (or supernatural) realm as Jesus intended.

Jesus was telling Nicodemus what John had described earlier, *But as many as received Him* [Jesus], *to them He gave the right to become children of God, to those who believe in His name: who were born, not of blood, nor of the will of the flesh, nor of the will of man, but of God* (John 1:12-13). Yet Nicodemus didn't understand because you can't understand spiritual things unless you have been born again by the Spirit.

Jesus answered, "Most assuredly, I say to you, unless one is born of water and the Spirit, he cannot enter the kingdom of God. That which is born of the flesh is flesh, and that which is born of the Spirit is spirit. Do not marvel that I said to you, 'You must be born again.' The wind blows where it wishes, and you hear the sound of it, but cannot tell where it comes from and where it goes. So is everyone who is born of the Spirit."

—John 3:5-8

Earlier we saw Moses face-to-face with God in the cloud at the tabernacle, and now here is Nicodemus face-to-face with Jesus (who is God in the flesh), right in front of Him, asking questions and reasoning with Him. But before Nicodemus even asked the first question, Jesus saw straight into him and said, "You must be born again." From that statement alone we can see that God is not impressed about how much we know. What He cares about is the condition of our heart.

SOME…CAN EVEN QUOTE THE BIBLE WORD FOR WORD, BUT THEY HAVE NOT BEEN BORN AGAIN IN THE SPIRIT.

If you are reading this book and you cannot remember a time when you truly were in God's presence, if you do not have that face-to-face opportunity with the Lord whenever you seek it, this is the question for you: *Are you truly born again? Do you really know God?* There are many people who would answer yes, and some of them can even quote the Bible word for word, but they have not been born again in the Spirit. What does that entail?

Our whole salvation experience is based upon John 3:16, in which Jesus said, *"For God so loved the world that He gave His only begotten Son, that whoever believes in Him should not perish but have everlasting life,"* and verse 18 which says, *"He who believes in Him is not condemned; but he who does not believe is condemned already, because he has not believed in the name of the only begotten Son of God."* Jesus wasn't talking about being raised in church and knowing all about God. He was talking about being born again by the Spirit of God and having a personal relationship with Him.

Remember, this is not about our flesh being reborn, it's about being born again in the Spirit. It's in the Spirit that we change and become a new creature because that's how all *old things...*[pass] *away* and *all things...become new* (2 Corinthians 5:17). Have you ever seen someone accept Christ who had a past life that wasn't exactly something they were proud of? It is as if all of a sudden they are changed. The change is so radical for some people, while for others, it is slower and happens over time—but it begins in the Spirit when they become born again.

Sometimes it's really disappointing when you hear people make fun of born-again Christians, or when some Christians don't want to admit that they have been born again because they are afraid of the world's reaction to them or they don't want to "offend" unbelievers. It is true that we live *in* the world, but when we are born again, we are not *of* the world (John 15:19), and we can draw close to God because we have His Spirit inside of us.

THIS IS NOT ABOUT OUR FLESH BEING REBORN, IT'S ABOUT BEING BORN AGAIN IN THE SPIRIT.

In the same way, if we are not born again, we are not Christians. We are not saved. We do not have the Spirit of God living within us. We are not His living tabernacle, and we will not be able to experience His presence. We are not going to know which way to go when we need to make a decision. We are not going to be sure of God's will. We are not going to understand His Word. In other words, we will not be able to enjoy any of His blessings.

My (Tonilee) husband was raised in a different faith (it was actually a cult). He is a very intelligent man who has read lots of books, articles, and other materials, and is a very comprehensive reader; he can always figure out what they're saying. Yet before he became a born-again Christian, he used to try to read the Bible, but he couldn't understand it. He just could not get it, and he didn't know what it meant. He thought it was crazy and would always end up closing it and putting it away. That changed when he came to know Jesus as his Lord and Savior.

IT IS ONLY BY THE SPIRIT THAT WE ...HAVE THIS INCREDIBLE SENSE THAT GOD IS WITH US IN THE EYE OF THE STORM.

When he believed in his heart that it was Jesus who died for his sins and that there was no other way to get to heaven—*not through good works, not through any other way but through Jesus Christ*—he received the Holy Spirit. From then on when he started reading the Word of God, he understood, for the first time, what he read.

Whenever we read the Bible, it is only by the Spirit that our minds are open to the things of God. It is only by the Spirit that we can bow down and worship the Lord and start to have this incredible sense that God is with us in the eye of the storm and that no matter what is going on around us, there is a supernatural peace and rest that can come in our hearts and minds.

Only when we are born again can we understand these things and know that we've been called to be set apart because God has a purpose and a plan for every single one of us. John 1:1,14 says that the Word (Jesus) was in the beginning and the Word became flesh and dwelt among us. Jesus came to earth fully God and fully man and He, himself, was filled with the Holy Spirit (Matthew 3:16) to accomplish the work determined by God the Father.

You can set up your tent outside the camp, you can spend hours in your closet and pray, but if you are not born again by the Spirit, you are only going to make yourself feel good for a moment. When the psalmist talks about tasting and seeing the goodness of the Lord (Psalm 34:8), he's talking about being in the life-changing, radical, amazing presence of the Creator of the whole universe. It is human nature to look for people to complete us, but the only One who can is God, when His presence, His Spirit, is in our lives.

Think of it this way: If Jesus himself tells us that we are physically born first of flesh, but we must be born of the Spirit (or in Jesus' words, "born again"), then it must be something important that He wants us to do.

How do we become born again? By believing in Jesus' finished work on the cross—knowing that we cannot have a relationship with the Father without the blood of Jesus making atonement for our sins—and by praying a simple prayer like this: *Dear Lord, I know I am a sinner. I know that You sent Your Son to die on the cross, shedding His blood for my sins. I ask You, Jesus, to come into my heart and save me. I surrender control of my life to You. Please fill me with Your Holy Spirit and lead me in Your ways. Thank You for saving me. Amen.*

BY ENTRUSTING OUR SPIRITUAL WELL-BEING TO CHRIST THROUGH FAITH, WE CAN TAKE HOLD OF ALL JESUS DID FOR US.

Believing in Jesus is as simple as that— we believe that God sent His Son, Jesus, who was fully God yet fully man, and He came down from heaven, born of a virgin, and entered this world to endure every temptation and have every opportunity to sin that is possible. Yet He chose a sinless life because He was God in the flesh, and He became the ultimate sacrifice for mankind.

When God did that out of love for us, it was to give every person the opportunity to accept Jesus as their Savior so that they too could enter the kingdom of God forever. So it's by receiving Jesus in our heart that we are born again and come to have a relationship with the Father, for John 14:9 says, *"He who has seen Me has seen the Father."*

What's in it for us, then? (Remember, it's okay to ask that). By entrusting our spiritual well-being to Christ through faith, we can take hold of all Jesus did for us (restoring our relationship back to God, which we'll cover later on) and receive all the fullness of the promises given from the beginning of creation. This all becomes possible the moment we accept Jesus as our personal Savior because we receive His Holy Spirit.

A DIFFERENT LEVEL OF COMMITMENT

Beyond accepting Jesus into your heart, the truth is, you cannot be in the presence of the Lord without the Spirit of God.

> *This is how we experience* [God's] *deep and abiding presence in us: by the Spirit he gave us.*
> —1 John 3:24 MSG

How do you receive the Holy Spirit? What happens when you receive Him? How do you embrace the Holy Spirit and His role in your life?

Now we want to take you further by laying a scriptural foundation of who the Holy Spirit is and how He affects you daily because you need this understanding in order to practice the presence of the Lord.

THE HOLY SPIRIT IS A DISTINCTIVE, DIVINE PERSON.

The Holy Spirit is a distinctive, divine person who is the third Person of the Trinity: the Father, the Son, and the Holy Spirit. (See Matthew 28:19.) He has existed since the beginning: *In the beginning...the Spirit of God was hovering over the face of the waters* (Genesis 1:1-2). The Holy Spirit does not draw attention to himself but without Him, we cannot understand the Bible for the Word of God was given to holy men by the Spirit (2 Peter 1:20-21), and is comprehended because of the Spirit. His works and presence are clearly seen and, at times, mentioned throughout the Bible.

In the Old Testament Scriptures, the Holy Spirit directed, guided, counseled, and instructed persons individually for the leading of the nation of Israel as a whole because it was through the nation of Israel that God laid a foundation for His purposes and plans to send His Son, Jesus, into the world for the redemption of sin.

The role of the Holy Spirit interacting with an individual differs from the Old Testament to the New Testament. The Spirit was continually active throughout history—He gifted the men to build the tabernacle, He filled men at times with the gift of prophecy, and He anointed David to be king of Israel among other things. But even though we learn of His presence in the Old Testament, the Spirit was not released fully at that time.

The Holy Spirit often came *upon* certain people, but He was not fully released to seal and empower individuals until after Jesus was glorified (John 7:39). You see, Jesus hadn't yet died on the cross, so God could not come to abide *in* people without the blood of Christ to cover them and cleanse them from their sins for that kind of relationship. God didn't indwell them until after Jesus was resurrected and ascended into heaven. When Jesus was glorified, He left us His Holy Spirit (John 14:16-17, 26) so that we may have and enjoy a personal and intimate relationship with the Lord.

IN THE OLD TESTAMENT SCRIPTURES, THE HOLY SPIRIT DIRECTED, GUIDED, COUNSELED, AND INSTRUCTED PERSONS.

We can't even call Jesus *Lord* without the Holy Spirit—there is a difference in saying, "I know Jesus" versus "Jesus is my Lord." That is a whole different level of commitment in our heart. The *Message Bible* says it this way, *His Holy Spirit, moving and breathing in you, is the most intimate part of your life, making you fit for himself.* (Ephesians 4:30). At that point we are guaranteed as partakers of the divine inheritance and sealed for eternity.

This seal of the Holy Spirit is like a stamp on the back of a letter. In ancient times, a king would place his seal on a letter, indicating that the letter was his and officially from him. Paul used the same word in Ephesians 4:30 (KJV) to describe what happens to us after believing and trusting in Jesus—we receive His seal of the Holy Spirit, guaranteeing that we belong to Him. We are sealed for eternity as His stamp is literally upon us. This seal means that nothing can separate us from the love of Christ (Romans 8:38-39) or from His divine inheritance (1 Peter 1:4)—but there's more.

Before Jesus ascended to heaven after His death, burial, and resurrection, He appeared to His disciples and told them, *"Peace to you! As the Father has sent Me, I also send you." And when He had said this, He breathed on them, and said to them, "Receive the Holy Spirit"* (John 20:21-22). That's all John says about this account, but Luke gives us further details on it.

> WE ARE SEALED FOR ETERNITY AS THE HOLY SPIRIT'S STAMP IS LITERALLY UPON US.

Luke 24:45 says that Jesus spoke with them and opened their understanding to the Scriptures, especially those concerning Him in the Old Testament. Then in verse 49 He told them, *"Behold, I send the Promise of My Father upon you; but tarry in the city of Jerusalem until you are endued with power from on high."* You may be wondering, *Who is the promise? What's up with the promise? What did Jesus mean?*

The disciples were happy, they were together, and they knew in their hearts that everything Jesus said is true—so what were they waiting for? This power from on high was the promise of receiving the Holy Spirit. The promise was given many years before by the Old Testament prophet Joel.

> *"And it shall come to pass afterward*
> *That I will pour out My Spirit on all flesh;*

Your sons and your daughters shall prophesy,
Your old men shall dream dreams,
Your young men shall see visions.
And also on My menservants
and on My maidservants
I will pour out My Spirit in those days."

—Joel 2:28-29

You can come to the Lord and then want to hang out in church and want to read the Word and want to have Christian friends, and you can become a blessing to each other; and that is exactly where the disciples were. They were sealed with the Holy Spirit, which is what we just learned about. But there was still something they needed.

The beginning of the book of Acts is a continuation, in a summary, of the end of Luke. We learn in Acts 1:3 that Jesus showed up on resurrection day and remained with the disciples for forty days, personally teaching and training them about things pertaining to God. Verse 4 says, *Being assembled together with them, He commanded them not to depart from Jerusalem, but to wait for the Promise of the Father…"* Didn't we just read the same words in Luke 24:49? Then Jesus said, *"which…you have heard from Me; for John truly baptized with water, but you shall be baptized with the Holy Spirit not many days from now"* (vv. 4-5).

When Jesus breathed on the disciples in John 20, they received the Holy Spirit, right? So now what are they waiting for? The baptism of the Holy Spirit, because it is something different, is something more. Jesus was saying to them in these verses, "When you received the Holy Spirit, your mind was opened to the Word, but now you are going to be baptized in the Holy Spirit, and you are going to receive power to be My witnesses." You see, there is a difference between being infused with the power that seals you for the day of redemption versus having that power living in you right now to make a difference in the world.

So what is the baptism of the Holy Spirit? When does it happen? Why does it matter to us today? If the Bible clearly tells us that we are the temple of the Holy Spirit, that God himself lives in each of us through His Spirit, then we need to know how to live like we believe it. Paul says in 1 Corinthians 4:20 that *the kingdom of God is not in word but in power.* The only way we can be empowered as Christians is to live a Spirit-filled life through the power of the Holy Spirit.

THE ONLY WAY WE CAN BE EMPOWERED... IS TO LIVE A SPIRIT-FILLED LIFE THROUGH THE POWER OF THE HOLY SPIRIT.

POWER TO CHANGE THE WORLD

At the end of forty days, Jesus ascended to heaven, but the disciples had to wait another ten days, until the day of Pentecost, to receive the power to be witnesses for Him in the world. If you study the Old Testament, you'll find the reason for that. You see, Pentecost is a Jewish feast that comes fifty days after the celebration of the Feast of the First Fruits.

Jesus was resurrected on the day of the Jewish Feast of First Fruits. Remember, Jesus hung out with the disciples for forty days, which meant they would have to wait another ten days for the Holy Spirit to fall on them—on the day of Pentecost.

When the Day of Pentecost had fully come, they were all with one accord in one place. And suddenly there came a sound from heaven, as of a rushing mighty wind, and it filled the whole house where they were sitting. Then there appeared to them divided tongues, as of fire, and one sat upon each of them. And they were all filled with the Holy Spirit and began to speak with other tongues, as the Spirit gave them utterance. And there were dwelling in Jerusalem Jews, devout men, from every nation under heaven.

—Acts 2:1-5

This passage goes on to say that these devout men were amazed because they heard the disciples speaking about God in the languages of these Jews. In verses 12-14 the Bible continues, *They were all amazed and perplexed, saying to one another, "Whatever could this mean?" Others mocking said, "They are full of new wine* [or they are just drunk]. *"But Peter, standing up with the eleven, raised his voice and said to them, "Men of Judea and all who dwell in Jerusalem, let this be known to you, and heed my words,"* and he went on to preach about Jesus. (vv. 15-36).

Since the ascension of Christ into heaven, this was the first sermon that was ever preached about Jesus Christ, about repentance, and about salvation—and it was the first message that was given under the power of the Holy Spirit. It was so effective that verse 37 says, *When they heard this, they were cut to the heart, and said to Peter and the rest of the apostles, "Men and brethren, what shall we do?"* Notice that it was no longer about the witnesses that were hanging out together *doing* church. It was now about the world and spreading the message of the Gospel to the lost and dying who had not recognized the Messiah for who He was.

This was Peter who was speaking. He had been the most outspoken of the twelve apostles. This was Peter, on whose faith Jesus himself had promised to build His church in Matthew 16:16-19. This was Peter, who Jesus had predicted would deny even knowing Christ in Mark 14:30. This was Peter, the disciple who did deny any knowledge of Jesus in Matthew 26:74-75. This was Peter, who hid in the Upper Room before Pentecost. This was Peter, the *...young man clothed in a long white robe...* (Mark 16:5) mentioned to the women at the garden tomb saying, *"Go, tell His disciples—and Peter—that He is going before you into Galilee; there you will see Him, as He said to you"* (v. 7).

This is Peter, who was now filled with the power of the Holy Spirit to preach a sermon that caused 3,000 people to come to Christ that day! Can you see how different these disciples are now? They are changing and the church is starting to grow.

The interesting thing here is that Peter goes on and says, *"Repent, and let every one of you be baptized in the name of Jesus Christ for the remission of sins; and you shall receive the gift of the Holy Spirit. For the promise is to you and to your children, and to all who are afar off, as many as the Lord our God will call"* (Acts 2:38-39). Who are those children Peter referred to? We are those children.

We are those generations that have come and today can testify of the Lord. Yet if we are not empowered with the Holy Spirit, we live in a place of guilt because we can't figure out why we have prayed for a certain person for several years but just can't tell them about Jesus. We live in a place of confusion because we don't understand why these trials are so hard and it feels as though we don't have the tools to get through them. We live in a place of frustration because we don't really know how to pray with confidence, so we just resort to praying, "Lord, I just want Your will to be done, and someday I will be in heaven and I will understand it." That is not victory. That is not power. It is defeat and martyrdom.

WE LIVE IN A PLACE OF FRUSTRATION BECAUSE WE DON'T REALLY KNOW HOW TO PRAY WITH CONFIDENCE.

If we are going to die, let's die for Jesus Christ. Let's not die hoping that we are saved and someday we will understand it all when we get to heaven. You know, we have such a short period of time on earth, and Jesus has promised that He has given us everything for life and godliness. He has promised that all power and authority have been given to Him, and yet we concentrate so much on the devil. We give him so much credit, when God has given Jesus the keys to death, hell, and the grave to give us eternal life—but eternal life doesn't start the day your heart stops. Eternal life needs to start today.

Today is a day of salvation. Today the Lord is calling each of us. Today the Lord wants to use us, but for some reason, we just praise and worship and show that we are Christians at church. When that happens, it remains a personal conviction and never becomes a public confession.

The truth is, it takes the power of the Holy Spirit in you to get you to the point of saying, "Jesus, don't let anything stop me from walking with You or being used by You, not even myself." That's when the Lord can really use you.

BUILDING BLOCKS
■■■■■■■■■

■ Question 1: Read John 1:10-13 to answer the following questions.
   a. Who is John describing in these verses?

   b. Who did Jesus come for?

   c. What was promised to those who believe?

■ Question 2: Read John 3:6-11 to answer these questions.
   a. How does Jesus describe the Spirit?

   b. Who is Jesus speaking of in verse 11?

■ Question 3: From John 3:1-12, answer the following questions.
   a. What "must" happen to have a relationship with the Lord?

   b. How does this happen? (See Romans 10:9-13.)

   c. By becoming born again, how do we understand heavenly things?

■ Question 4: How have you personally viewed the Holy Spirit in your life? Take time to write down your comments, perceptions, and questions about Him.

Chapter 3

EVIDENCE OF RELATIONSHIP

The Fruits and Gifts of the Spirit

I (TONILEE) CAME TO KNOW THE LORD WHEN I was fourteen because of my mom. She became born again and then she kept telling me for two weeks straight, "You have to know Jesus; it will change your life." My mom's life had already changed so much (in a good way) that I was afraid to accept Jesus in my heart because I thought I could lose her somehow. In my way of thinking, I had already lost her to this Christianity thing.

Although we felt we were Christians because we went to church every week and believed in God, I also was afraid because I knew it would be a commitment. My mom had changed so much that I knew this could happen to me too, and I didn't know if I could live with myself like that, let alone live with her this way. Finally one Sunday before church, I went upstairs, got down on my knees, and quickly prayed "Okay, God, if You want me, You need to show me."

I got up from my knees and we then left for church. To my surprise, the minister started his sermon by saying, "Why are you afraid to accept Jesus Christ as your Lord and Savior? This message is being said for all those who are afraid." At first I was stunned. Then I turned to my mom and said, "I can do it now." Right then, I bowed my head in the pew and gave my life to Jesus, and the power of the Holy Spirit came in and began to change me.

I came to know the Lord personally and I loved praising God. Joy just filled my heart, and I wanted to read the Bible all the time, which was a big change because I had never cared about reading it before. One of my friends noticed the changes in my mom and me, and about five months after I had accepted Christ, she asked me to go to a retreat with her at another church. We had never been a part of another church before, but my mom said I could go.

During a communion service at this retreat, I felt the presence of God so strongly that I said to Him, "Lord, I will do anything for You. I will go anywhere for You. Use me however You want." I didn't realize it at the time, but that's when I completely surrendered to God—not only "Jesus, I believe; I want to go to heaven," but now "Jesus, use me. Send me. Take me." There's a difference between the attitude of "I'm doing this for me" (to go to heaven) versus "I want to live for You" (bringing heaven to earth). I also sensed something I have since heard called *liquid love* or a feeling like hot oil is being

THERE'S A DIFFERENCE BETWEEN THE ATTITUDE OF "I'M DOING THIS FOR ME" VERSUS "I WANT TO LIVE FOR YOU."

poured on you. It was the love of God enveloping me as I came into His presence and surrendered my will.

We're going to look at the fruit of the Spirit in a moment, but the Bible tells us in Galatians 5:22 that His first fruit is love. Seeing the evidence of God's presence in your life begins with knowing and understanding that He loves you and wants to have a relationship with you. The more we give ourselves to God, the more we sense His love. That's the role of the Holy Spirit in your life—to enable you to enter into God's presence and to empower you to live in victory.

The Spirit of God dwelling within you is like receiving an engagement ring from God. God gave us a promise that we will one day be united with Him and married to Him forever, and 2 Corinthians 1:22 says that [He] *has sealed us and given us* [His] *Spirit in our hearts as a guarantee.* The result of this promise should be seen as evidence of His Spirit in your life.

THE SPIRIT OF GOD DWELLING WITHIN YOU IS LIKE RECEIVING AN ENGAGEMENT RING FROM GOD.

How can your life bear witness to the presence and power of the Holy Spirit living within you?

Once the Holy Spirit has empowered you and is in charge of your life, then you should see changes in your life through His fruits and His gifts—both are evidence of God's presence in you. You may already know about the fruits and gifts of the Spirit, but we're going to look at them next to see how we reflect them when we live our lives in an active relationship with the Lord through the power of His Spirit.

EVIDENCE OR INCIDENTS

How do we visibly see the presence of the Holy Spirit working in our lives? We cannot physically see the wind, but we can see evidence of the wind as trees are blown and sounds are made because of its forces. The same is true of the Holy Spirit. We cannot see Him physically, but we should be able to see evidence of His works in our life. In fact, our desire should be to see this evidence every day, but so often we just see glimpses or incidences of Him.

The word *evidence* is used seven times in the Bible, six in the Old Testament book of Jeremiah and once in the New Testament book of Hebrews. The prophet Jeremiah used the word *evidence* as a form of writing like a scroll, documenting proof of something being recorded. Hebrews 11:1 uses *evidence* as something that proves or tests our faith. In essence, *evidence* is proof that something exists, and as Christians there should be proof that the Holy Spirit lives within each of us.

REMEMBER, YOU CAN'T ENTER HIS PRESENCE WITHOUT THE HOLY SPIRIT.

One way to examine this evidence or proof is by examining the fruit of the Spirit within your own life. Fruit is manifested through the conduct of our lives, not just sporadically but consistently. Basically, when you're spending time in God's presence, you're going to bear fruit. Remember, you can't enter His presence without the Holy Spirit, and He is the One who produces the fruit. Jesus used the fruit tree, or the vine, as a wonderfully descriptive analogy to help us better understand this.

> *"For a good tree does not bear bad fruit, nor does a bad tree bear good fruit. For every tree is known by its own fruit. For men do not gather figs from thorns, nor do they gather grapes from a bramble bush."*
>
> —Luke 6:43-44

Jesus told us in these verses that we should be as a tree that bears good fruit, and just as He said here that a tree is known by its fruit, so are we known by our fruit. Keep in mind that the tree will need to experience seasons of cold frost and painful pruning, but the goal is to bear fruit. Living a life empowered by the Spirit means that you will experience similar seasons with the same goal and purpose in mind—to be a fruit bearer. He leads, guides, instructs, exhorts, and He also corrects us on how to live out the truth in our everyday lives to please the Lord.

Fruit is an interesting kind of concept because the *fruit of the Spirit* [in a Christian life] *is love, joy, peace, patience, kindness, goodness, faithfulness, gentleness and self-control* (Galatians 5:22-23 NIV). There is one condition, though, to living a fruitful life: As Christians, we can't bear fruit apart from Jesus.

Some Christians can look really good—they come to church, get involved, serve in different ministries, volunteer, and never miss a Sunday. Then there are people (some in other religions) who would like to call themselves Christians. Many of them are good, moral, upstanding people who live good lives. Many of them look much more spiritual than I ever feel. But they are like fruit that looks really good, but only on the outside.

THEY ARE LIKE FRUIT THAT LOOKS REALLY GOOD, BUT ONLY ON THE OUTSIDE.

I (Bobbye) heard Billy Graham talk about fruit one time. He told how his wife kept a beautiful bowl of plastic fruit on their kitchen table, and so often he would come into the house and grab an orange to eat from that bowl. He thought it was real because outwardly it looked like fruit, but it didn't take long for him to realize that there was nothing on the inside of it. This is how we are when we're not spending time in God's presence. On the outside we can look like we have the good fruit of the Spirit—shiny, pretty, doing all the right things—but if we're not abiding in the Lord, we're going to bear bad fruit. Let's look at a beautiful illustration that Jesus gave about the evidence of abiding in Him to show us the life we should be living as Christians.

ABIDING IN THE VINE

In John 14, Jesus was giving His farewell message to His disciples because it was almost time for Him to go to the cross. They didn't really know it was His farewell message, but He was having His last words with them and He was saying good-bye. He told them about the Holy Spirit, the Helper, whom He was going to send to them when He went to be with His Father in heaven (vv.16-17). Then He said, *"He who has My commandments and keeps them, it is he who loves Me. And he who loves Me will be loved by My Father, and I will love him and manifest Myself to him"* (v. 21).

Now the word *manifest* here is very similar to *evidence*. It means "to show, to make appear, to place before the eyes so that an object may be seen."[1] Jesus was saying that He was going to give them evidence of himself by showing himself to them—to "be a real and spiritual Presence to the obedient and loving believer."[2]

That was difficult for some of the disciples to understand and one of them, Judas (not Iscariot) asked Him, *"...Lord, how is it that You will manifest Yourself to us, and not to the world?"* (v. 22). In other words, how was Jesus going to do that through the Holy Spirit? Jesus answered, *"...If anyone loves Me, he will keep My word; and My Father will love him, and We will come to him and make Our home with him"* (v. 23). Think of it: the Trinity—the Father, Son, and Holy Spirit—coming to live with us and making their home in us.

WHEN JESUS DIED, HE BROKE THE BARRIER BETWEEN SINFUL MAN AND A HOLY GOD.

These disciples had been with Jesus for three years. They were personally trained by Him, but at this point the Holy Spirit—this Helper whom Jesus was talking about—did not live in them. That's why it was so important for Jesus to die on the cross. When He died, He broke the barrier between sinful man and a Holy God. And since Jesus' death and resurrection, we have been able to receive God in us, which is what the Holy Spirit is. But that wasn't all Jesus promised them.

> *"Peace I leave with you, My peace I give to you; not as the world gives do I give to you. Let not your heart be troubled, neither let it be afraid."*
>
> —John 14:27

Jesus not only promised us peace, which is one of the fruits of the Spirit, but He said that He's going to give us peace because He's abiding or living in us. Abiding is the key to experiencing His presence in our lives and bearing good fruit.

Some Bible scholars speculate that Jesus then left the Upper Room and started walking through Jerusalem toward the Brook Kidron. At that time the vine was a symbol of Israel. A replica of it was actually etched in the stone wall of the temple where everyone could see it. Jesus may have been walking by the temple with His disciples and happened to look up and see the carving of the vine there when He told them, *"I am the true vine, and My Father is the vinedresser"* (John 15:1). Actually, He was saying that Israel was a symbol of the vine, but He is the real Vine. Then He explained the significance of the vine in our lives.

> ABIDING IS THE KEY TO EXPERIENCING HIS PRESENCE IN OUR LIVES AND BEARING GOOD FRUIT.

> *"Every branch in Me that does not bear fruit He [Father God] takes away; and every branch that bears fruit He prunes, that it may bear more fruit. You are already clean because of the word which I have spoken to you. Abide in Me, and I in you. As the branch cannot bear fruit of itself, unless it abides in the vine, neither can you, unless you abide in Me…He who abides in*

Me, and I in him, bears much fruit; for without Me you can do nothing.... If you abide in Me, and My words abide in you, you will ask what you desire and it shall be done for you.... You did not choose Me, but I chose you and appointed you that you should go and bear fruit, and that your fruit should remain, that whatever you ask the Father in My name He may give you."
—John 15:2-5,7,16

Can you see from this passage the answer to our problems? It is in a relationship that develops from abiding with Jesus. We need to abide in Him to deal with the things in our lives that keep us from the presence of the Lord, and that is what His Holy Spirit does in us—He makes that relationship possible.

ABIDING IS RESTING. IT'S AN INTIMATE AND PERSONAL RELATIONSHIP.

The word *abide* in the Greek translation has several definitions. They all basically mean the same thing—to "stay" or "dwell" or "remain"[3] or to adhere to—and that is how we need to be in our relationship with the Lord, in a place of abiding.

Abiding is resting. It's an intimate and personal relationship. Abiding means that you don't need to figure out what to do to work for God because you can't do it apart from Jesus. Otherwise, your fruit (good works) may look good on the outside, but there'll be nothing on the inside. It is in that place of being connected to God's Vine (Jesus) that He will do the work through you.

I (Bobbye) have read about a vine in London that is over a thousand years old. The amazing thing is that it has been there so long it has roots and a trunk that literally are like a tree, and it's still growing and thriving. The reason it has lasted so long is it gets enough water and is protected from certain environmental elements. It can weather certain storms because the roots of that vine go deep into the ground, and the vinedresser makes sure there's soil and it's fertilized and everything is right for that vine to grow. He watches over it, keeps it, and is the gardener, the tender, of it. As a result, branches come up and grow forth from the vine.

So it is for every Christian. Psalm 1:3 and Jeremiah 17:8 talk about the tree planted by the river. When I (Bobbye) read how that tree (or a vine) is planted and those roots go deep, and its water source is like a river flowing into it, I thought of the Holy Spirit flowing His living water into our lives.

What a wonderful depiction of the power and grace that Jesus used to describe His Holy Spirit flowing through us.

> *"If anyone thirsts, let him come to Me and drink. He who believes in Me, as the Scripture has said, out of his heart will flow rivers of living water."*
>
> —John 7:37-38

The river of living water represents life, but the river that has no flow or movement can represent the opposite, a body of water that is lifeless and dead. Which one represents your life today?

Jesus is the only One who has the living, life-giving water. His love is the force behind the waters that give them power and strength and is evidenced through His Holy Spirit, who fills us to overflowing like a river overflowing its banks. Because of the living water, we bring life to everything around us; just as a river supports an enormous amount of animal and plant life, we can also give support to others in our lives. The reason is that where we go, Jesus goes and His Spirit goes with us. That's why a kind word or gesture from us can taste as sweet as water to a thirsty soul.

JESUS IS THE ONLY ONE WHO HAS THE LIVING, LIFE-GIVING WATER.

Jesus also said, *"I am the vine, you are the branches"* (John 15:5). Jesus is our Vine, our water Source, and just as the branches have to be connected to that grapevine or they have no life, we as the branches must be connected to the Vine, Jesus, or we have no spiritual life. We are connected when we abide in Him. Would you agree that this is a relationship that is definitely adhered to?

WE AS THE BRANCHES MUST BE CONNECTED TO THE VINE, JESUS.

In real life, as with the grapevine, the branch doesn't have a choice. It has to stay connected to the vine because that is its lifeline. The branch doesn't say, "I'm just going to pluck myself off the vine today," or "I'm going to go over here, vine; I'll be back and plug into you again later when I'm hungry," but Christians do that all the time. Then they wonder why they have only an occasional moment or incident of fruit instead of a continual evidence of fruit in their lives.

Jesus tells us that if we want to bear fruit, we must continue abiding with Him because He is our lifeline—He's the air we breathe, He's the only water we need, He is our food beyond physical food, He's our only hope, He is everything we need! The end of the branch is where the fruit grows, but the branch does not produce this fruit. It comes from the vine. In other words, without the entire relationship, no fruit is going to be produced.

Everything in this process of maintaining the condition of this vine has to do with abiding—the vine being alive, the branch being connected, and then the fruit coming forth. That should be the goal for our lives—as we are in that abiding relationship with Jesus, we will bear much fruit because the presence of the Holy Spirit is in our hearts.

PRODUCING GOOD FRUIT

Are the fruits of the Spirit evident in your life or do they appear as incidents?

We each struggle with fruit production. For some, self-control is the hardest; for others, patience is the greatest challenge. Regardless of our weaknesses, all Jesus asks is that we are willing to confess our struggles and allow Him to work within us as He wills because fruit is not produced naturally. It is the work of God as the believer yields to His work in their lives.

God often works in our lives through difficult people, unpleasant circumstances, and challenges of life events by using them to change us, yet many Christians refuse to see His hand in these terribly difficult situations. While God doesn't cause the difficulties, He often uses them to place limits and boundaries on our flesh so that we have to rely on His help to bear the fruits of the Spirit.

The trouble we sometimes have as Christians is not being able to distinguish God's work from the circumstances. Instead, we become frustrated, angry, and overwhelmed, and begin to doubt that God is with us at all. We focus on the people and events instead of submitting to the Lord through them. We sometimes fail to understand that God is in control and that He allows these things to happen to test and try us to grow us up spiritually and emotionally because He loves us. (See Psalm 26:2; 139:23.)

> WE FOCUS ON THE PEOPLE AND EVENTS INSTEAD OF SUBMITTING TO THE LORD THROUGH THEM.

That is part of the Christian life, so instead of whining and moaning and groaning and complaining to everybody about what we're going through, we need to learn to do what God tells us in His Word and learn about the kind of relationship He wants us to have with Him. It's a two-way street.

Submission to the Lord is a recurring theme that you are going to see throughout this book. The reason is that in order to experience His presence in your life, it is critically important to submit to Him, trust in Him, and to stop resisting His purposes. Of course, if someone is asking you to do something against God's Word or restricts you from doing what God has commanded, then you obey God, not man. But for the most part, God uses all things (including people and circumstances) and works them together for your good (Romans 8:28) when you are abiding in Him.

Good fruit bearing happens when you submit and trust the Lord for every detail of your life, like praying, "Lord, what do You have for me in this?" instead of praying, "Why, God, why?" or "When, God, when?" Many times the "why" and "when" kinds of prayers happen because our flesh does not want to believe that God would allow us to feel so uncomfortable. And those why and when prayers can be indicators that we are fighting against submitting to God and trusting that He knows and sees all that affects us. This behavior prevents the Holy Spirit from working within us and will ultimately result in fruitless efforts.

IT IS GOD'S WILL FOR YOU TO HAVE…MORE LOVE, JOY, PEACE, PATIENCE, KINDNESS, AND THE OTHER SPIRITUAL FRUITS.

The way to develop fruit is by praying, "How, God, how? How can I be pleasing to You in this? How can I bear fruit? How can I love You better? How can I bring You glory?" It is God's will for you to have a little more love, joy, peace, patience, kindness, and the other spiritual fruits through whatever comes across your path. That is living the victorious Christian life. It's not about the people or circumstances changing; it is about you changing with the people and the circumstances to reflect more of God's character.

The fact is, the tighter the squeeze on your flesh, the greater you will see what pops out of your mouth from your heart—whether it's good fruit or bad depends on you.

THE GIFTS OF THE SPIRIT

My (Tonilee) teenage son, Robby, is really into the sport of tennis, and recently he said to me, "Mom, I just want to live for tennis. I want to play it every day, and I want to take lessons to get better, so I don't understand why you can't take me to do this all the time." I told him that we all need a balance because there are many things his dad and I would like to do all the time too—like teach the Bible, write about the Bible, and talk to people more often about the Lord. When he heard that, his face dropped and he said, "You can't do that! Who would take me to my tennis lessons? And who would pay for them?"

It was very clear to Robby why my husband and I needed a balance in our lives, but it wasn't clear to him why he needed a balance in his. As we continued to talk, I told him his sisters had goals that they wanted us to do for them too, and that we are a family of five, who all have different roles and jobs and functions; but the goal is to be one and to work together as one. He could see that better, especially when I explained that this is what the Lord says to believers, particularly in the realm of spiritual gifts.

GOD WANTS US TO BE BALANCED IN OUR CHRISTIAN LIVES.

God wants us to be balanced in our Christian lives, but there will be times when we will lose that balance. God has a way of keeping that balance in us, if we stay sensitive to Him, and He does that through the fruits of the Spirit. When we come to Jesus, we believe that He's the Son of God, and we receive the Holy Spirit. At that point we get that big "C" (for Christian) on our forehead; then we take the next step and ask for the power of God from on high, and He empowers us with gifts of the Spirit to perform the works for the body of Christ, manifested with the fruits.

You may be familiar with the spiritual gifts listed in 1 Corinthians 12:28 and Ephesians 4:11, but they generally fall into two categories—they're used for testimony (witnessing to others) and for service (doing everything as unto the Lord).

- *Service/Equipping*—apostleship, prophecy, discerning of spirits, teaching, the word of knowledge, the word of wisdom, speaking in tongues, interpretation of tongues.
- *Sign/Testimony*—workings of miracles, gifts of healings, ruling and governments, helps.

We have broken that down into four divisions: (1) *Service Gifts*—apostles, prophets, evangelists, pastors, and teachers; (2) *Sign gifts*—healings and miracles, tongues and interpretation of tongues; (3) *Supporting Gifts* (that help those who are in service)—administration, exhortation (which is coming alongside someone to lead them closer to the Lord), giving, leadership, mercy, and service; and (4) *Stewardship Gifts*—wisdom, knowledge, discernment, and faith.

OUR GOAL IS TO BECOME ONE IN THE BODY OF CHRIST.

We are all given at least one gift and some of us are given many gifts, but as we pursue the presence of God and walk this path with Him, the goal is to become one in the body of Christ to lift up the name of Jesus. It doesn't necessarily matter what gift you have as long as you are serving the Lord and working together in His body of believers.

As the body is one and has many members, but all the members of that one body, being many, are one body, so also is Christ.
—1 Corinthians 12:12

The apostle Paul is comparing the gifts of the Spirit here to the members of our physical bodies. Each member has a function that is necessary for the health of the whole body. Eyes give sight, ears are for hearing, legs are for walking, lungs give us the ability to breathe, and even our big toe is necessary for balance. Removing one piece would hinder the function of the whole body. The truth is that the Holy Spirit distributes the spiritual gifts to the members of the body of Christ (v. 11) for the same purpose—to ensure that the body functions as a whole, healthy unit. If one member suffers, then the whole body suffers. If one member rejoices, then the whole body rejoices.

Paul is saying that we need to come together as a group and learn how to serve each other to make this body work effectively, in order to spread the Gospel of Christ. That's really one of the main reasons why the gifts were given. They are not only for the equipping of the saints, the building up of the body for the ministry (Ephesians 4:12), and for our everyday life. They are given so we can share our faith with others to bring more souls into the kingdom of God, and serve the Lord better by the things that He does through us. Then the glory goes to Him.

> WE NEED TO COME TOGETHER AS A GROUP AND LEARN HOW TO SERVE EACH OTHER TO MAKE THIS BODY WORK EFFECTIVELY.

So these gifts are not of us or from us, but they are from God to be used for His purposes.

> [God] *handed out gifts of apostle, prophet, evangelist, and pastor-teacher to train Christians in skilled servant work, working within Christ's body, the church, until we're all moving rhythmically and easily with each other, efficient and graceful in response to God's Son, fully mature adults, fully developed within and without, fully alive like Christ.*
>
> —Ephesians 4:11-13 MSG

Too often spiritual gifts are highlighted by the individuals who claim to have them, but spiritual gifts are not given for our personal benefit, nor are they meant to draw attention to ourselves. No one owns their gift. The Holy Spirit does, and He gifts those whom He wills for the purposes determined by God. As we practice His presence, *He* works within us so that others in the body will be edified, lifted up, encouraged, healed, and exhorted. The power belongs to Him, as we are mere vessels used as He directs us to perform the work of the ministry.

Even though I (Tonilee) have certain gifts to use for the Lord, sometimes as I'm walking through this Christian life, I come up against opposition, and I feel as if I'm walking against the wind.

AS WE PRACTICE HIS PRESENCE, *HE* WORKS WITHIN US SO THAT OTHERS IN THE BODY WILL BE EDIFIED.

I've asked the Lord at those times, "How come, Lord, how come?" He continually reminds me, "You need a balance, Tonilee. If you just run off and play tennis or do whatever else you want to all the time, you might forget that over here, somebody needs to be ministered to. And you're not going to have the self-control to stop to hear My voice and follow Me if I tell you to change your direction." See, spiritual gifts and the fruit of the Spirit go together.

You may be wondering what your gifts are. I didn't know what my gifts were for twenty years! People would tell me what they saw in me, but all I knew was that I loved Jesus and if there was a need, I would say, "Here I am, Lord, send me." For instance, if my church needed a house opened for a meeting, I'd say, "Lord, will You give me the ability to open up my house for that?" and He would.

It is the same for everyone in the body of Christ—the more you make yourself available to the Lord, the more He will equip you with any gift you need for His glory. When you just want to serve Him with all your heart, He will give you whatever you need. Then the gifts become about the Lord and not about us.

So far we've used the Word of God to lay a foundation—that is Jesus and the Holy Spirit and His power—to show you what it takes to enter into God's presence. Once you receive Jesus as your Lord and Savior and you are filled with the Holy Spirit, you have everything you need for the very victory that He has promised you, and you have all the fruits and gifts that stem from having that intimate and personal relationship with Him.

As you go through the process, though, remember that you are going to grow and mature. The question for you today is: do you want to look back on your life and see only occasional incidences of peace, of love, of joy, of blessing others, or do you want your life to be one of continual fruit bearing and operating in the spiritual gifts? Seeing this evidence of God's presence in your life begins with knowing and understanding His love for you, knowing that no matter what happens in your life, He is in control and you can trust Him and rest in Him.

IT DOESN'T MATTER HOW MUCH IS GOING ON AROUND YOU...IF YOU ABIDE IN GOD'S PRESENCE, YOU WON'T BE DISCONNECTED FROM THE VINE.

It doesn't matter how much is going on around you. The wind can blow, things can happen on the surface, but if you abide in God's presence, you won't be disconnected from the Vine. You'll be abiding in Him and see continual fruit and gifts in your life—it will be a life of victory, a life of His Spirit in you, a life that from then on, will flow out of you to bless others. When you really start to see God's full picture of His plan for His church and how He can use you for the body of Christ, then your relationship with Him will become even more beautiful and the blessings even greater.

BUILDING BLOCKS
■■■■■■■■■

■ Question 1: What evidence is seen in your life that bears witness to the presence of the Holy Spirit working within you?

■ Question 2: Rank the fruits of the Spirit in order from most to least as evidenced in your personal life.

■ Question 3: The goal of the Christian life is to "bear much fruit" (John 15:5-8). Write a personal prayer asking the Lord to help you in the weakest areas of your fruits.

■ Question 4: Read John 15:1-8 to answer the following questions.
   a. What part of the Vine do we represent?

   b. What must happen before fruit is borne? (vv. 4-5). Give two reasons from verse 8 for why we should bear much fruit.

   c. What pattern or cycle of circumstances prevents you from bearing fruit?

■ Question 5: Read Ephesians 4:30 and 1 Thessalonians 5:19 to answer these questions.

   a. What are we doing to the Holy Spirit when we refuse to allow the Lord to have His way in our lives?

   b. How have you grieved or quenched the Holy Spirit in your life? Give an example.

Chapter 4

ALL ABOUT *ME* OR
ALL ABOUT *GOD*?

The Struggle to Live in His Presence

THE PRESENCE OF GOD IS OURS. HE LOVES US beyond our understanding. By His great love, mercy, and grace, He chooses us and wants to dwell with us continually, and He has made a way for that to be possible—He sent His Son to die for us so that He could live inside of us through His Holy Spirit. So why aren't more Christians experiencing His presence in their lives every day?

Some people say, "It can't be me. I'm not doing anything wrong." Others say, "It's all my fault. I'm in sin, and I can't get any victory," or "Whenever I go to the Word, I don't understand it," and they end up in this eternal struggle of not knowing where their role starts and where God's role ends. We have written this book to deal with these concerns and to cast light on the reason for the struggle—the battle between the flesh and the spirit.

I (Bobbye) came to Jesus when I was a child. I actually accepted Jesus into my heart and prayed the prayer of salvation more than once, so I've known most of my life that He lives in my heart. However, as I grew up, I was always very strong willed and very controlling in the sense that I wanted things in my life to be a certain way—my way.

For years I had very specific and intense ambitions and desires and goals for my life. Now there's nothing wrong with that if they are in line with the Lord's plan for you, but my position was always me first and God would have to come alongside.

I was living a carnal life. There were things that I wanted to achieve that were driving my flesh, yet I wanted the Lord to help me to do them. I knew His Holy Spirit was within me and that He heard and answered my prayers; I knew I could pray for His protection and care; but I was being driven by my flesh, not by God. In spite of all that, God was so good to me—He never left me, and He was patient with me as I kept going down that path. The struggle inside of me, though, didn't bring me peace.

WHENEVER WE PUT OUR FLESH AHEAD OF GOD, WE ARE NOT GOING TO HAVE PEACE.

Whenever we put our flesh ahead of God, we are not going to have peace, even though God is with us and He *"will never leave you or forsake you"* (Hebrews 13:5). That's what I was doing as I pursued a career and everything else that I wanted.

Even though the Lord was with me, I was driving my life in such a way that, in a sense, I was always having the Lord catch up from behind. Instead of letting the Holy Spirit lead me and surrendering to what God may have wanted me to do, I was always jumping ahead, telling Him, "I'm going to do this, Lord, so come along and bless me."

God knows us and loves us so much that He will let us live like that—for awhile. But the time will come when we reach a place in our plans that we will know we need to understand God's desires for us and follow them. We will realize that the reason He wants us to be in His presence is to experience His peace. The struggle shouldn't always dominate our lives—we shouldn't always have to learn through our trials—even though God can use the struggle in our lives to mold us and shape us into the persons He created us to be.

Looking back, I realize I brought on so many of my circumstances myself. Can you relate to that? I would have times in my life where I would come back to church after a long absence and start to get involved again and know that the Lord was bringing me into the secret place of His presence that Psalm 91:1 talks about. I hate to admit it, but the truth is that I would intentionally walk away from Him because I would find that in living His way, I was moving away from my plans and goals for my life.

I would tell myself, *I'm going to church too much. How much am I willing to really let go and let the Lord take control over my life?* I would compare it to the heat of a flame getting a little bit too hot—I would find myself in God's presence, wooed into that place with Him by the Holy Spirit, but then I'd pull back and just disappear. I'd back off and stop going. My logic was, *I don't want to get too far out there away from my plans because my life might change. I'd better pull back.*

> HE WANTS US TO BE IN HIS PRESENCE TO EXPERIENCE HIS PEACE.

The point is, I wouldn't be here writing this book or be in ministry with Tonilee if my life hadn't changed. There definitely came a day when my flesh and my spirit lined up with what God wanted for me, and He could have His way in my life. Since then, I've learned that there's no other place I want to be but in His presence. There's no other way I want to live but in surrender to Him. Even though I still struggle with my flesh and with all those desires and issues in my flesh at times, my prayer every day is that I'm not led by them but that I'm led by His Spirit.

Now I didn't start in that place. I had to learn through a series of struggles and troubling events in my life. They finally made me realize that nothing is worth what I was going through to try to make my desires happen. There's no peace in that place, even though God is still with us. Living without peace is a sure sign that we are not coming into His presence daily.

THE LORD WANTS TO WALK WITH YOU IN FELLOWSHIP AND FRIENDSHIP.

There are reasons that we struggle with experiencing the presence of God, and they involve the components just mentioned by Bobbye that are in each of us. I'm (Tonilee) going to look at each of them with you right now because when you know what the problem is, you can ask the Holy Spirit to help you in those areas.

The Lord wants to walk with you in fellowship and friendship. He desires for you to agree with Him, submit to Him, and allow Him to set the course for your life. Once you learn how to end your struggle, you can be sure that you will like what God does with your life.

IT'S AN ONGOING BATTLE

The *first* component we all struggle with is our body. We each have a physical body that is made up of our physical structure, but our body is not the real us—it's not who we really are. Our body has to do with pain and pleasure, and it has issues. Our body gets headaches, it gets sick, it gets hungry, it has involuntary reflexes as much as voluntary reflexes. Our body brings us to certain places that affect our walk with Christ.

For instance, when you are dealing with illness, you may wonder, *Did God give this to me because I sinned?* Or, *Is God allowing this illness to happen in my life because He needs my attention?* Or, *Is this illness a thorn in the flesh because I'm too puffed up with pride?* Regardless of the reason, we deal with struggles because of the issues our bodies bring into our lives.

The *second* component we deal with is our soul. It is made up of three parts—our mind or intellect, our will or our desires, and our emotions or our feelings. Our intellect or our mind involves what we think: *Do I think I'm right? Do I think I'm wrong? Do I think I'm good? Do I think I'm bad? Where do I want to go with those thoughts?* Our emotions involve our feelings: *How do I feel? I feel good today. I feel bad today. I feel like reading the Bible. I don't feel like reading the Bible. I feel like getting up and being nice to my children. I don't feel like I want to do that this morning.* Our will involves the question, *What do I want?* For instance, *If I got a new car, maybe I would be happier. If I had certain desires and wants that were fulfilled, maybe that would fill the void in my life.*

So how we think, how we feel, and what we want really determine who we are and what we do. We end up being what we think, what we want, what we desire, what we are—all those things go into our soul, that part of us that we cannot see but really makes up who we are.

> HOW WE THINK, HOW WE FEEL, AND WHAT WE WANT REALLY DETERMINE WHO WE ARE AND WHAT WE DO.

The body and the soul together are the elements of a word in the Scriptures that is called the *flesh*. Before we come to Christ, the flesh is all about *me*, and as we saw in what Bobbye shared earlier, the flesh doesn't leave us when we become born again. It is one of the antagonists in our struggle.

The *third* component that makes up each one of us is our spirit. We were created in God's image and so we are given a spirit when we are born into this world, but because of the fall in the garden with Adam and Eve, we are born into sin. Our spirit is literally dead because it's not alive to the things of God until we become born again.

We have a choice to make because our soul and our body continually have to choose which way they want to go—whether to follow our flesh or our spirit. Since we are born of flesh, our natural tendency is to go the way of the flesh, which is why Paul talked about the battle that is raging in each of us. (See Romans 7-8.) The important part, however, is that our choices will have eternal repercussions.

Until we come to Christ, we are separated from God. If we don't come to Christ at all, we will be eternally separated from God. Our spirit will live on when our physical flesh (our body) dies—either in heaven or in hell. This is where the struggle really takes place, between our spirit and our flesh.

The truth is that even though we are both spirit and flesh before we come to Christ, there's not as much of a battle going on between the two because we're not trying to walk with the Lord. And our enemy, Satan, has his claws on us. He blinds us to the things of God, so we don't struggle as much between spirit and flesh. But remember that before we come to Christ, the Holy Spirit is still wooing us to come to Him. There is a battle of sorts going on for those who don't yet know the Lord—for those people the Holy Spirit is trying to bring into the kingdom of God. You may not realize this, but even in their rejection of the calling of God on their lives, there's a struggle taking place on the inside of them.

THE STRUGGLE BETWEEN OUR BORN-AGAIN SPIRIT AND OUR FLESH...IS A CONTINUAL CONFLICT.

After we come to Christ, that struggle intensifies, and that's what Bobbye and I are really talking about in this chapter because every believer is going to have a struggle to practice the presence of God as a Christian. The conflict between our born-again spirit and our flesh in these earthly bodies that is "all about me" is a continual struggle.

If a desire or a want becomes your complete motivation in life, then your whole purpose becomes a struggle to go in that direction.

The struggle in itself is the battle we deal with that can keep us or hinder us from building an intimate relationship with God.

Those who live according to the flesh set their minds on the things of the flesh, but those who live according to the Spirit, the things of the Spirit. For to be carnally minded is death, but to be spiritually minded is life and peace. Because the carnal mind is enmity against God; for it is not subject to the law of God, nor indeed can be.

—Romans 8:5-7

This term *carnally minded* refers to the struggle with our flesh that we feel as Christians when we are in the middle of the battle between our flesh and our spirit. It's also very similar to a word used in James 1:8—*double minded.* When you come to Christ, all you want is Jesus. You may be like I (Tonilee) was—every time the pastor gives an altar call and prays the prayer for people to accept Christ, you are praying that prayer too.

So you are at that place where your heart is saying, *I just want to love and serve the Lord. I just want more of God.* But your mind is saying, *I'd better not do that. What if I get tested in this and I don't like what God does?* Or, *Wait a minute. I don't have time to go to church on Sunday mornings. I can still spend time with God without going there every week.* Here's what's happening when you find yourself at that point.

Your mind is putting you in a place that's completely different from—which doesn't make sense with—your heart, so your heart is at one place and your mind is at another. If you think about it, it's just twelve inches between your ears that is causing all this conflict. In other words, you're being carnally minded.

To give you the big picture of what it means to be carnally minded, we are going to take you back to the story of Adam and Eve because it is the best example of carnally-minded persons in the Bible.

We often hear people say that Adam and Eve are to blame for this whole creation mess, and that's absolutely true. But, remember, we are made in God's image, and He knows that if each of us were presented with the same circumstances and situations, we would have followed the same path. Adam and Eve represent all the choices every man and every woman would have made if we were in exactly the same situation.

HOLD ON TO FAITH, NOT FEAR

In the beginning of the book of Genesis, the Lord began to talk about how He created the heavens and the earth and how He created man. Everything was okay for the first two chapters; they were all about God. Then everything changed in the third chapter when Adam and Eve fell, and the rest of the Bible is all about winning us back.

God had clearly laid a foundation for man by saying, "You can eat from every tree in the garden except one." (See Genesis 2:16-17.) If you recall, God had put two trees in the center of the garden— one was the tree of the knowledge of good and evil. The other was the tree of life—and God told Adam and Eve not to eat from the tree of the knowledge of good and evil. Now they had the rest of the Garden of Eden to roam around and they had plenty to eat and to do there, until Satan (or Lucifer, the devil—the Enemy) showed up and started having a conversation with Eve.

Now the serpent was more cunning than any beast of the field which the LORD God had made. And he said to the woman, "Has God indeed said, 'You shall not eat of every tree of the garden'?" And the woman said to the serpent, "We may eat the fruit of the trees of the garden; but of the fruit of the tree which is in the midst of the garden, God has said, 'You shall not eat it, nor shall you touch it, lest you die.'" Then the serpent said to the woman, "You will not surely die. For God knows that in the day you eat of it your eyes will be opened, and you will be like God, knowing

good and evil." So when the woman saw that the tree was good
for food, that it was pleasant to the eyes, and a tree desirable to
make one wise, she took of its fruit and ate. She also gave to her
husband with her, and he ate.

—Genesis 3:1-6

Can you see how clever the Enemy was to get Eve to follow her fleshly desires instead of being led by the Spirit? She said she saw that the fruit was good, it was pleasant to the eyes, it was desirable, and it was going to make her smart. Her flesh desired to try it because it looked like good food, so why not take a bite?

Until that point, Adam and Eve had enjoyed a wonderful relationship with God. God would walk in the garden, call out their names, and they would hear Him and come into His presence and fellowship with Him, but that all ended the moment they followed their flesh and disobeyed the Lord. The moment they took a bite of the fruit that God had told them not to eat, they died spiritually and became alive to the things of the flesh—and for the first time ever they lost their peace and felt fear.

God was walking in the garden the day they ate from the forbidden tree, and He called out their names, but their eyes had been opened in a new way, and they knew they had done something wrong. So this time they said, "Oh no, the Lord is coming," and they went and hid themselves from His presence because now they understood the difference between right and wrong—and they knew that they had done something terribly wrong.

The sad thing is that Satan knew exactly what to say to Eve to get her to follow her flesh instead of her spirit. He had told her, "God just doesn't want you to be like Him," but there was nothing further from the truth. God created Adam and Eve in His image. He wanted them to be with Him and enjoy complete fellowship with Him. But the Enemy stopped that by telling Eve that God was withholding something from her and tempted her to disobey Him. As a result, sin entered into the world, and so much fear entered into Adam and Eve that they were severed from the presence of God from that moment on.

I (Tonilee) noticed that when I started walking with the Lord, the Enemy often used fear to keep me from continuing to be in God's presence. I would fear surrendering my life to God. I would fear the future or fear to make a change. Then I read what the apostle Paul said about fear, *God has not given us a spirit of fear, but of power and of love and of a sound mind* (2 Timothy 1:7), and I understood for the first time that fear is not of God. To embrace fear is to choose against God.

PAUL WAS SAYING FEAR IS THE OPPOSITE OF POWER, THE OPPOSITE OF LOVE, AND THE OPPOSITE OF A SOUND MIND.

In that passage Paul actually was saying that fear is the opposite of power, the opposite of love, and the opposite of a sound mind. So I realized that if I continued to hold on to fear, I could lose the very presence of God, and I didn't want this because I knew that more of God means a better life.

When you become fearful, it's as though Satan is lying to you back in the Garden of Eden, and he's telling you that this fear is going to defeat you. You can't accept his lies because if you hold on to them, then you won't be in faith, and you will have a hard time coming into the presence of the Lord and receiving all that He has for you.

You may truly want to practice the presence of God, but you know there are issues of fear that are holding you back. You can pray for the fear to leave, but the best way to handle it is to work through fear with the Lord, beginning with being honest with Him about the things you're holding on to in fear. I've (Tonilee) had to learn to give everything to the Lord that can prevent me from walking with Him continually. I don't want any fear to take hold of me so greatly that I quench His presence, because once you have tasted being in the presence of God, you just want more and more of it, and there's no other place that you would rather be.

The Enemy used fear to sever Adam and Eve from God's presence, but God is so good because He already had devised a plan to restore mankind back to himself. That's one of the great things about the Word of God. The whole Bible is about restoring us back to the presence of the Lord.

We hope by now you are beginning to understand how much God wants you to be in His presence. You need to know that. You need to hear it often. You need to believe it— *God wants you in His presence.* The problem is, you may not always want Him.

> THE WHOLE BIBLE IS ABOUT RESTORING US BACK TO THE PRESENCE OF THE LORD.

From the rest of Genesis on is the story of God's people, the children of Israel, whom He chose by His sovereign will to be His own people. Ultimately Jesus would be born from that line, but the Old Testament is filled with proof that time after time God went out of His way for His people. How many times did we see God do absolute, divine, supernatural miracles to demonstrate His presence to them, yet they turned away from Him. Let's look at the book of Exodus again and see more ways that God revealed himself to His people.

AN ATTITUDE OF INGRATITUDE

Exodus was the book written by Moses to really tell the story of how the Israelites escaped from Egypt. We see story after story in Exodus of what God did for the children of Israel after He used Moses to lead them out of Egypt and Egyptian bondage—miraculous things like parting the Red Sea, giving them water when there was no water, giving them manna or bread that literally came raining down from heaven, and instructing Moses to build a tabernacle so that God could dwell among them. It just seemed that no matter how many miracles they saw God do, in their flesh they still dealt with the issues of fear, worry, doubt, and unbelief. Isn't that indicative of how many Christians are today? At least the Israelites had an excuse.

Remember that in the Old Testament before Jesus came, the children of Israel didn't have the Holy Spirit to indwell them as we have, but He would be with select people at various times. God himself came down and dwelt in the tabernacle that Moses built just to be with these people.

God's heart, then and now and forever, has been and always will be that He wants to be with us. Yet even though we have God's presence within us, we need to understand that God wants us to be in His presence continually, and that no matter what we do against Him, He still wants us and loves us. The Israelites didn't understand this, and they ended up with the attitude of ingratitude.

When God would perform a miracle for them, initially they would respond with excitement and praise for what He did: "Oh, isn't God great? We went through the Red Sea on dry ground. He's brought us water from the rock." But before long they would start to complain again.

GOD'S HEART, THEN AND NOW AND FOREVER, HAS BEEN AND ALWAYS WILL BE THAT HE WANTS TO BE WITH US.

One time that happened right after the Israelites came through the Red Sea and God had wiped out their enemies. When they reached the other side, they started singing a song about how great God is (Exodus 15), but their praises were short-lived. Just a little while later they said to Moses, *"Oh, that we had died by the hand of the LORD in the land of Egypt, when we sat by the pots of meat and when we ate bread to the full! For you have brought us out into this wilderness to kill this whole assembly with hunger"* (Exodus 16:3). They had become miserable, and so quickly!

What a complete picture of their hearts being with God, but their minds ending up taking them away in a different direction. Their spirit, the center of their heart, was going, "Yes, we are with God, we are crossing this Red Sea, we are out of Egypt," but their minds allowed that attitude of ingratitude to come in and cause them to forget all that God had done, and it became all about the flesh and "What about me?"

Again in Exodus 19:8 we see their hearts. The Bible says, *Then all the people answered together and said* [to Moses], *"All that the LORD has spoken we will do."* So one minute it was, "Yes, we're with You, God," and the next minute it was, "What, is He crazy? Look how uncomfortable I am; I don't want to do that," and then it was back to, "Praise the Lord!"

Before you judge them too harshly, keep in mind that there's a big difference with the Israelites in the book of Exodus and who we are today and why we can have victory over our flesh when they couldn't.

Sometimes we wonder why we can't see the kind of miracles God performed for the children of Israel thousands of years ago. We want to see the Red Sea part today. We want to see God rain down food for us from heaven this evening. Yet they saw miracles happen and they still complained and rebelled and refused to come into His presence. We know that at the end of this story most of that entire generation roamed in the wilderness for forty years

WE WANT
TO SEE THE
RED SEA PART
TODAY.

and never made it to the Promised Land because of their hardened hearts and rebellion. But we have an advantage over them.

We saw earlier, in the story of Nicodemus, that we can be born again because Jesus went to the cross and died for us. In the Old Testament, the Israelites had many rituals for the atonement of sin, like killing animals, including a pure spotless lamb (symbolic of

Jesus) that had to be sacrificed, even during the Passover[1] feast. The reason was that they didn't have the blood of Jesus to cleanse them from their sins or the indwelling of the Holy Spirit to empower them to come into God's presence.

It wasn't until the New Testament that Jesus became that pure, spotless sacrifice for us once and for all. For those of us who accept Him as our Savior, we immediately receive the Holy Spirit—the One who enables us to enter in and remain in the presence of God continually. Where the children of Israel struggled so much in their hearts and minds in the Old Testament, today we should be together in our hearts and minds because we have the indwelling of the Holy Spirit to help us to train our minds as well as change our hearts.

PUT OFF, PUT ON, AND PUT AWAY

> *You should no longer walk as the rest of the Gentiles walk, in the futility of their mind, having their understanding darkened, being alienated from the life of God,...because of the blindness of their heart.... But you have not so learned Christ, if indeed you have heard Him and have been taught by Him, as the truth is in Jesus: that you put off, concerning your former conduct, the old man which grows corrupt according to the deceitful lusts.*
> —Ephesians 4:17-18, 20-22

The apostle Paul is saying here that you need to put off that flesh part now, and in the next passage, he continues, *Be renewed in the spirit of your mind, and that you put on the new man which was created according to God, in true righteousness and holiness. Therefore, putting away lying, "Let each one of you speak truth with his neighbor," for we are members of one another* (vv. 23-25). You may be looking at those verses and wondering, *Okay, how do I do all that?*

You could wake up in the morning and say, "Today I'm not going to sin," but that is not realistic. The bridge between putting off (v. 22) and putting on (v. 24) is verse 23 that says to be renewed in the spirit of your minds and also verse 25, which talks about putting away our former conduct. God is able to strengthen you to change and redeem your old ways into a new person with ripe, healthy, abundant fruit, but there are things you need to put off, put on, and put away that you can only do through being renewed by the spirit of your mind.

That is the reason why we want so much to show you the difference between your heart and your mind—to help train your mind to think differently by thinking in the Spirit and not in the flesh.

We know that you are reading this book because you have a heart for God, and that is necessary if you are to live in His presence. King David had a heart for the Lord and was also able to be victorious in doing the things God had asked him to do. Yet many Christians today have a heart for the Lord, but they don't have those fruits He promised. They don't understand how to pray in order to see Him answer their prayers the way Jesus promised. They don't have that peace that Jesus not only left as a fruit, but also promised He'd give us in the world.

We are sure you don't want that kind of life, and we don't want that for you. We want to help you to understand the presence of God so you can tap into a life that brings you daily victory, regardless of the circumstances, because the goal of the Christian life isn't that we're going to be trouble free. If anything, when we get born again, we become more aware than ever before of the battle of the flesh and the soul versus the spirit.

GOD IS ABLE TO STRENGTHEN YOU TO CHANGE AND REDEEM YOUR OLD WAYS INTO A NEW PERSON.

The problem is, we get this false impression of the Lord that once we come to Him, everything should just be great, and if it isn't we tell the Lord, "If You love me, this shouldn't happen to me." Yet the Lord tells us in His Word that it will.

"Fear not, for I have redeemed you;
I have called you by your name;
You are Mine.
When you pass through the waters, I will be with you;
And through the rivers, they shall not overflow you.
When you walk through the fire, you shall not be burned,
Nor shall the flame scorch you.
For I am the LORD your God,
The Holy One of Israel, your Savior."

—Isaiah 43:1-3

Things are going to happen to you as a believer just as much as they're going to happen to a nonbeliever. The Bible says that the rain falls on the just and the unjust alike (Matthew 5:45). The difference is that the Lord wants you to know His presence is always there with you. I'd (Tonilee) rather go through trials walking with Him than go through a trial without Him and wonder what I am doing wrong.

THE CHRISTIAN DEALS WITH THE SAME ISSUES THAT THE NON-CHRISTIAN DEALS WITH, BUT THE DIFFERENCE IS THAT WE HAVE JESUS.

The Christian deals with the same issues that the non-Christian deals with, but the difference is that we have Jesus. The other difference that He wants you to know is that He's going to take you by the hand and cause the terrible thing to work together for good (Romans 8:28). I'm not saying that the terrible thing is good. God doesn't put terrible things in our life to say, "I can work it out for good now." No, He says, "These things are going to happen, but I'm going to be with you in it, and you're going to see how I can make something beautiful with this mess."

The issue is we have to be willing to go with Him instead of fighting Him. Instead of asking, "Lord, why are You doing this to me?" we have to be able to say, "Lord, I know You're still here." It involves training our minds to think differently as we go through troubles so that as we're walking through the fire or feeling like we're drowning in the water, or walking through the valley of the shadow of death, the fruits of the Spirit are not quenched in our life. We're still enjoying the love of God, and we're still experiencing the joy of the Lord that's becoming our strength, and we're still finding peace in the midst of the storm.

This is what makes you different as a believer from the unbeliever who is dealing with exactly the same issues, and it is the goal of the Christian life—that we live in that place of victory and peace.

EVEN AFTER
WE BECOME
BORN AGAIN,
WE ARE NOT
YET FULLY
MATURE IN
THE LORD.

A WHOLE NEW WORLD

If your life reflects more of following your flesh than your spirit, don't feel bad. Before we come to Christ, we are going to follow our soul, but even after we become born again, we are not yet fully mature in the Lord, and there may be times when we want a certain thing so we train our minds to follow right along with our wants or with what we feel.

Actually, they can work together, but sometimes they can also just completely pull you apart. We showed you one illustration of that at the beginning of this chapter through Bobbye's story. I (Tonilee) had the opposite issue but still dealt with being pulled apart by it.

When I came to Christ as a teenager, I understood the presence of the Lord right away and how He can empower you to do unbelievable things for Him. I was very excited about Him and didn't ever want any of that quenched.

When I was fourteen, I was getting my medical assistant's license and by sixteen, I was working in hospitals very comfortably in that position. I even traveled to different hospitals that needed me. By the time I was twenty-one, I had graduated from nursing school and was very comfortable working in a hospital and with sick people. Eventually, I began to work in a very progressive, aggressive hospital. The hospital administrator there must have observed my comfort level in spite of my young age, because within three months, I was asked to apply to become the charge nurse of their extremely intense neuro-ortho ward.

Now a registered nurse who only recently passed the Boards shouldn't really have been in this head position, but they saw that I was comfortable in that setting and had the ability to handle the job, so I started pursuing that administrative nursing career.

When I wanted to be promoted to a new position, I would pray about it, and every time I would get the promotion. I continued to be promoted, but it got to a point where I felt like they were making up excuses to promote me. Soon I began to think, *Maybe I'm becoming so earthly minded that I'm not spiritually good anymore.*

You've probably heard the saying, "You're so spiritually minded you're no earthly good"? Well, in this case I flipped it around because I was pursuing this career in the hospital and enjoying all the financial blessings and positions of power that I suddenly received with the promotions. I was now hiring and firing people who had been in the field so much longer than I had been, and I started thinking that this couldn't be God's will.

So instead of facing Bobbye's situation of being a Christian who was putting her flesh first and letting God follow, I was the opposite. I understood what it was to be so Spirit-led that I couldn't accept the blessings I was receiving in the world—blessings of promotion and position. I couldn't figure out how the two went together so I quit pursuing the administrative ladder and ended up in ICU instead, but the same thing happened there.

I started climbing the same ladder of promotion, but again my spiritual maturity wasn't at a place where I could accept both the blessings that God gives through these things and practicing His presence. It took some time and spiritual growth, but eventually I saw that God was in all of it because my heart was in the right place with Him.

Whether you can relate to Bobbye's kind of situation or mine, if you love the Lord so much that you're aware the minute you are doing something that quenches the Spirit, then you might want to quit what you're doing. But you know what? Had Joseph done that, the Israelites would have been in really bad shape. If Daniel had quit, King Nebuchadnezzar would have been in a completely different place. You have to reach a certain level of spiritual maturity to be able to accept the earthly blessings of the Lord while not quenching the Spirit of God—and understanding that His presence is continually with you regardless.

The point of our two illustrations is to give you two ends of the spectrum to let you know that walking with the Lord is a learning process. I (Bobbye) think it's funny that both of us even came together because we have such different stories. In my case, I was driven by my flesh and wanted to follow my own path until I reached the place where I realized I needed to be led by God, not Him following me. In Tonilee's case, all she wanted to do was be led by God's Spirit, and then when she was led by Him, she had trouble accepting what He was doing in her life out in the world.

> THERE'S A MATURITY THAT COMES AS YOU CONTINUE TO SEEK HIM.

God will use everything in your life for your good and His glory, but we were both spiritually immature in certain ways and didn't understand this at first. There's a maturity that comes as you continue to seek Him, and there's a balance in your walk with Him as you enter into His presence everyday. Then it becomes less about some of the details your flesh wants to focus on and more about lining up whatever you're doing and whatever your desires are with what God is calling you to do.

How is it possible that you can be in the presence of God like this? No matter where you are, no matter what you do, you cannot escape the Lord. He's always with you. King David wrote a beautiful Scripture passage about it.

> *Where can I go from Your Spirit?*
> *Or where can I flee from Your presence?*
> *If I ascend into heaven, You are there;*
> *If I make my bed in hell, behold, You are there.*
> *If I take the wings of the morning,*
> *And dwell in the uttermost parts of the sea,*
> *Even there Your hand shall lead me,*
> *And Your right hand shall hold me.*
>
> —Psalm 139:7-10

If you don't remember anything else of what we've said so far, we hope that you have come to know how much God loves you and wants you to be in His presence. Just as He chose the Israelites to be His people, by His great mercy and grace, He chooses you today. He loves you beyond your understanding, and He has plans for you beyond your imagination that He wants to share with you as your relationship with Him grows more and more. It's just a matter of training yourself to live in that place of being in His presence continually every day because He's always with you.

HE HAS PLANS FOR YOU BEYOND YOUR IMAGINATION THAT HE WANTS TO SHARE WITH YOU AS YOUR RELATIONSHIP WITH HIM GROWS.

Part of developing any relationship is through getting to know the other person. The Bible clearly tells us of God's character so when we spend time with Him and in His Word, we can learn more about who He is and begin to understand Him better. For example, God is love. God is righteous. God is faithful. God is perfect in every way. God is all-knowing, all-powerful, and ever-present. He cannot be anything but who He is, and He will never cease to love you or let you down because He can't go against His nature.

To help you to grow and mature in becoming a daily disciple of God, we are going to address the ways to practice the presence of God in the rest of this book. As you put these truths into practice, you will get to know who the Lord is and who He wants to be in your life—and a whole new world will open up to you. That's how we want to live our lives, and we're thankful that it's how you want to live yours.

BUILDING BLOCKS

■ Question 1: Have you ever experienced being in the presence of the Lord? Why or why not?

■ Question 2: What three components make up each of us that cause us to struggle with being in God's presence? How have they affected you in practicing the presence of God?

■ Question 3: From Genesis 3:1-10, answer these questions.
   a. What happened to Adam and Eve after they ate of the forbidden tree?

   b. Why weren't they able to come into God's presence?

   c. Have you ever done something that kept you from experiencing God's presence? Explain.

■ Question 4: The enemy used fear to keep Adam and Eve from God's presence. What is the best way to handle fear?

■ Question 5: Read Exodus 15; 16:3; 19:8 to answer these questions.
   a. How would you best describe an "attitude of ingratitude"? Why do you think the Israelites had that kind of mind-set toward God?

   b. What does the Holy Spirit do to help us to train for victory over our flesh?

■ Question 6: Read Ephesians 4:17-18, 20-25.
   a. What is the bridge between putting off "the old man" and putting on "the new man"?

   b. Do you think in the Spirit or in the flesh? Explain.

■ Question 7: What are some differences between Christians and non-Christians who are dealing with the same issues?

Chapter 5

THE MOST INCREDIBLE PLACE TO BE

Practicing the Presence of Worship

O NE OF MY (BOBBYE) SISTERS HAS AN ELEVEN-year-old son named Aaron. For some reason, Aaron loves classical music. He can't get enough of it. Even when he rides in the car, he has his headphones on, listening to the music of Mozart and Beethoven and other great classical composers. Aaron wants to play classical music so he's taking piano lessons and learning to sight-read the notes as well as to play by ear. My three sisters and my mom were visiting me recently, and my sister who is Aaron's mom was telling me something amazing about Aaron. He will practice the piano for hours, and she actually has to go tell him to stop practicing.

I don't know about you, but I've known many parents with children who wanted to take piano lessons, but the parents wouldn't necessarily have to make them stop practicing. It's more like they would have to force their child to practice, even just for ten minutes. Parents generally have to beg, plead, and do whatever it takes to get their child to practice with that type of commitment, but Aaron practices the piano for hours because he loves it.

Whenever we do something because we love to do it, it is really not about practice at all. It becomes a way of life. If we could even begin to grasp in our hearts a desire to practice worshiping God like Aaron practices that piano—because we love it—imagine what our lives would be like.

Worship is our truest, deepest, most sincere form of expression of our love for the Lord. We were created for worship, and we will spend eternity worshiping Him. Did you know that worship is only meant to be for God?

> WORSHIP IS OUR TRUEST, DEEPEST, MOST SINCERE FORM OF EXPRESSION OF OUR LOVE FOR THE LORD.

John, the author of the book of Revelation, was actually being shown end-time events that are to come. At the conclusion of the book, in chapter 21, he saw the final heavenly city where those of us who are going to heaven will be one day. And he was just amazed by what he saw taking place there.

An angel stood before John and he began to bow down before this angel to worship him, but the angel rebuked John and said "No, don't worship me. I am a created being. I am a fellow servant like you. Worship God. He is the only One to be worshipped." (See Revelation 22:8-9, author paraphrase.)

If I were to ask a group of people what they thought worship meant, they'd probably each have a different answer. That is a big question, and I believe there are many concepts and misconceptions about it, but when we put the word *practice* in front of *worship*, all of a sudden it has a whole different twist.

It's one thing to practice the presence of God, which can be difficult to conceptualize, but how do we practice the presence of worship?

So often we think of the word *practice* in connection with things that we need to get better at, as an athlete practicing his sport or a musician, like my nephew, practicing his instrument. In this chapter you are going to see worship as not just singing a few songs or coming to a church service or however else you may define worship, but as something that you practice every day of your life—with all your heart.

Let's begin with some basic facts about worship: (1) worship only counts when we worship God, and (2) worship is not only about singing and verbal expression, but it's about what we do with our whole being and every part of our lives all day long.

IMAGINE WORSHIPING GOD IN EVERY BREATH YOU TAKE—THAT'S TRUE WORSHIP.

Imagine worshiping God in every breath you take—that's true worship. It's not giving God a couple of minutes of your time when you first get out of bed in the morning before you start your day or before you go to bed at night. Worship needs to be practiced throughout your day in the same way that you would practice anything you love to do. God has to become much bigger in your mind for your issues to seem a lot smaller so you can trust Him with them. This trust comes from learning how to worship.

The word *worship* is first mentioned in the book of Genesis when God told Abraham to take his beloved son Isaac to Mount Moriah to offer him as a sacrifice to the Lord (Genesis 22:2). Abraham obeyed and told his servants that he and the boy were going to the top of the mountain to worship God (v. 5). The Bible says that at the last moment God stopped Abraham from sacrificing his son because He saw Abraham's heart of worship and obedience (v. 12).

So from the beginning, acts of worship were not always associated with acts of singing and praise. Sometimes worship is simply an act of sacrifice.

A MATTER OF THE HEART

Therefore, I urge you, brothers, in view of God's mercy, to offer your bodies as living sacrifices, holy and pleasing to God—this is your spiritual act of worship.

—Romans 12:1

The apostle Paul wrote these words, talking about the mercies of God (we're all here by God's mercy and grace) and presenting our bodies as a living sacrifice to Him. What does that mean, and what does it have to do with worship? This passage actually refers to how the system of worship was set up in the Old Testament.

WHAT IS IN OUR HEARTS TENDS TO BE WHAT COMES THROUGH OUR ACTIONS AND BEHAVIORS.

We learned earlier that we are made up of three parts: (1) the physical body that we all can see; (2) the soul, which is our mind or intellect, our emotions, and our will or desires; and (3) our spirit, which can't be seen but is eternal and will live forever in either heaven or hell. These three components make up what we have been given to express our worship to God. Worship comes through our body, through our mouth, through our words, through our behaviors and more often than not, through what is in our hearts. We're going to take a look at what is in our hearts because that tends to be what comes through our actions and behaviors.

When we read Paul's words about presenting or offering our bodies (our lives) to God as a living sacrifice, we tend to associate *sacrifice* with something negative or something that was done in the Old Testament. The fact is that when Paul spoke these words, Christ had died on the cross, risen from the grave, and ascended into heaven. Paul was starting to establish his churches. So why would he talk about *sacrifice* in the New Testament, and why would he describe it as a form of worship?

We weren't born into this world with a desire to worship God. From the point when Adam and Eve fell into sin in the Garden of Eden and separation occurred between God and man, everyone who has been born was born with flesh. Flesh has a desire to sin. To be honest, all we really want to worship is ourselves, other people, and things that take precedence over God in our lives. We may not always know that we're calling it worship, but we are born with a desire to take care of us first. That desire continues even after we know the Lord and we give our lives to Him. It's something we battle with even after we're born again.

WE WEREN'T BORN INTO THIS WORLD WITH A DESIRE TO WORSHIP

God knows us so well, and He always looks at the depths of our hearts when He looks at us for worship because even though He alone is worthy to be worshipped, He chooses to have a relationship with us. This can be seen in the lives of Cain and Abel, who were born to Adam and Eve after they fell in the Garden of Eden. (See Genesis 4.) This is the first story in the Bible where someone brings an offering to the Lord, and it gives a clear picture of how we are as human beings. We tend to look at the outward appearance, but God looks into the depths of our heart to see what our true motives are.

No doubt you know the story of how both Cain and Abel brought a gift to God as an offering to honor Him. Abel brought a firstborn lamb from his flock. What did he do with it? He sacrificed it by killing it and giving it as an offering to the Lord. Remember, at that time, those kinds of gifts were considered a form of worship.

Cain also brought God an offering, but his was different than his brother's. Cain brought fruit or grain from his crops, and the Bible doesn't say that he brought the first fruit. It just says that he brought an offering from the field (v. 3). God looked at Abel's offering and it was pleasing and acceptable to Him, but He was not pleased with Cain's offering, and He rejected it.

You may be thinking, *What was the big deal? Abel brought God something and Cain brought God something. Why was God displeased with Cain?*

The reason is that it was a matter of the heart.

When God told Cain that He wasn't accepting his offering, it was because Cain didn't bring his first fruit to the Lord and what he did bring wasn't being offered from his heart. Not only that but many biblical scholars agree that it also was because Cain didn't bring a living sacrifice to God.

Abel brought something that was alive, and he laid it down before God and actually took its life as a sacrifice. It takes a piece of your heart to sacrifice before the Lord the life of something that you've raised and seen alive. Plus, it was a type of living sacrifice that was slain for Abel's sins, representing the Lamb of God—Jesus—who would eventually come and be slain on the cross to take away the sins of the world.

Cain still brought his offering to God, but God's rejection and rebuke caused his countenance to fall immediately, and he ended up murdering his brother out of anger and jealousy. What do you think God was looking at? He was looking at Cain's heart, and He knew what Cain was going to do before he did it. Abel's sacrifice came from the depth of his heart, while Cain merely offered his gift of fruit to remain on good terms with God.[1]

The story of Cain and Abel is reflected in the book of James, which talks about being double minded (1:8) and later describes double mindedness in 4:17, saying that if our soul knows the good it ought to do but can't align to the good (in thoughts, feelings, or goals), then it becomes sin. That was Cain's problem. Being double minded steals our joy, quenches our peace, and questions God's love, and it can cause us to sin. That is why worship is often associated with sacrifice. Our flesh will worship our own desires and pleasures before worshiping the Lord.

Coming before our God with a true heart of worship is represented by a heart that is surrendered to His will and not our own. We find the place of freedom in releasing to Him the people, things, and circumstances that tend to take hold of us. When we can do that, God can greatly bless us. To truly worship the Lord, then, we must make that sacrifice to put aside our earthly desires and to be willing to change how we think, how we feel, and what we want. This is why the Lord asks us to be His living sacrifices.

> BEING DOUBLE MINDED STEALS OUR JOY, QUENCHES OUR PEACE, AND QUESTIONS GOD'S LOVE.

WORSHIP THE ONE TRUE GOD

As time went on, God chose Abraham and through him created a whole nation of people for himself (Genesis 12:1-2). God set them apart from the rest of the world by telling Abraham to take his family and servants and leave Ur of the Chaldees (Abraham's hometown, located in modern-day Iraq, south of Baghdad). Then God began to teach them how to worship Him.

God had to establish the practice of worship in their lives because they had lived in a land of idol worshipers, filled with people who were worshiping forbidden, worthless gods. Much later His people would end up living in Egypt in bondage and slavery for over four hundred years and be exposed to Egyptian culture, false religion, and false gods. So He had to begin His relationship with them by teaching them to worship the one true God.

We read earlier about the story of the Passover lamb, another very critical part of sacrificing for worship. During the time God was preparing His people to be led out of Egypt by Moses, He told Moses about one of the last plagues that would take place to cause Pharaoh to allow the children of Israel to leave. God instructed Moses to tell the people that He was going to send an angel of death and that all the firstborn, people and animals, were going to be killed in the houses, even in Pharaoh's house. But God made a way of escape for the Israelites.

God said to Moses, "I want each of you to go and find a one-year-old lamb that's spotless and unblemished. You're to take that lamb into your homes and on the fourteenth day of the month (four days later), you're to sacrifice the lamb. You're going to kill it and smear the blood of that lamb (one lamb per household) on your doorposts so that the night the angel of death passes by, he will pass over all those places" (See Exodus 12.)

Just imagine having a little baby lamb in your home for four days and then laying it down and sacrificing it. It must have been heartrending, but it was done every year after that as the Israelites celebrated the Passover annually for generations, and they were still celebrating it when Jesus came.

As the story goes on in Exodus, we know that later Moses was told by God to build a tabernacle, which gave more of an established form of worship. God taught them how to practice worshiping the one true God by establishing rituals for them to follow. If you look at the book of Leviticus, you will see one after the other of different types of offerings, sacrifices, and celebrations that God instructed them to perform.

You'll also notice that He established the tabernacle with a court-yard around it. The biggest item in the courtyard was the altar for the burnt offering, also known as the bronze altar. It was the first thing the people saw when they came into the courtyard, and it was placed there so they could freely offer up an animal that would be sacrificed on that altar. Then they would burn the sacrifice on it for the remission of their sins.

At that time there was no other way to be forgiven of sins. So from their hearts, they would bring a live animal offering to God that had to be sacrificed and die as a symbol that their sins were forgiven by God. These practices were established throughout Israel for generations to come.

We know that Joshua, not Moses, ended up leading the children of Israel into the Promised Land. Some time after Joshua passed away, David, and then Solomon ruled over the Israelites and continued these practices for worshiping God. But at times the people were ruled by kings who did not follow God and His statutes, and the children of Israel worshipped false idols which pulled them away from God and caused them to do things that He had taught them not to do.

LEFT ON OUR OWN, WITHOUT PUTTING GOD FIRST IN OUR LIVES, WE'RE BOUND TO PUT VALUE ON THE WRONG THINGS.

You may be wondering why they would stop worshiping the Lord and turn to worshiping false gods when they had been taught God's ways of worship, and it had been so ingrained in them for so many generations. It's human nature. Left on our own, without putting God first in our lives, we're bound to put value on the wrong things and worship someone or something else because we were created for worship. It's a need that we have to fill one way or another.

Some people think that worshiping other gods means having actual statues or idols that we bow down to. Although many religions today do use such physical idols in their worship practices, most Christians do not associate with such activities, but the gods and idols many of us worship are not necessarily statues or images.

Idols are those things in our lives that take priority over our worship of the one true God. Idols can be people, places, things, and activities, or anything that controls us like fear, money, power, control, toys, or self-image.

People were no different in Bible times. They found ways to worship something and please themselves too. That's why throughout the Old Testament God established specific worship practices for His people so they would know to do them whether they were ruled by good kings or bad. Generation after generation followed these worship practices, including the Passover celebration, until for many of them it became a religious ritual that they worked themselves.

PEOPLE ARE ALWAYS WILLING TO TURN TO SOMETHING OTHER THAN GOD TO GET A QUICK ANSWER.

They knew exactly what to do and the right ways to do it, but somewhere along the line by the time Jesus showed up, the Pharisees—the most religious, ritualistic, practicing group there was at that time—had no more heart for God, and they were leading God's people in the same direction.

The Pharisees had no idea who God was. They were just going through the motions of worship, doing all the things the Law told them to do, but focusing their true worship on their position, their wealth, on people with social status—on everything but where it truly belonged. They had no desire or understanding of how to put their whole heart into worshiping the Lord because they didn't really know Him personally.

People are always willing to turn to something other than God to get a quick answer or to feed their desires in some other way when they are not seeking Him every day with all their heart. That was going on when Jesus came.

WORSHIP IN SPIRIT AND TRUTH

There's a story in the Old Testament about Samaria and how it came to be a nation of people of mixed races, and thus a forbidden place to the children of Israel. The Israelites were a pure nation that didn't marry outside of their race, and they wouldn't even walk through that land, let alone talk to a Samaritan—until Jesus came into the world.

Being Jesus, He went everywhere, and during His travels, He stopped at a well one day to rest and get refreshed. While at the well, He met a woman who came there at midday to fill her water pots (John 4:7). It just so happened that this woman had several past husbands, and the man she was living with now wasn't her husband—and she was a Samaritan.

Yet Jesus was having a conversation with her and not only that, He was telling her about what she had been doing in her life. She realized that this was no mere man, and she called Him a prophet. Then she said, "[Jesus,] *our fathers worshiped on this mountain, and you Jews say that in Jerusalem is the place where one ought to worship*" (v. 20). In other words, she was asking Jesus which was the right place to go to worship, but Jesus answered her, "*The hour is coming, and now is, when the true worshipers will worship the Father in spirit and truth*" (v. 23). What did Jesus mean by that?

WE DON'T HAVE TO GO TO THE MOUNTAIN OR TO THE TEMPLE IN ORDER TO WORSHIP HIM.

In essence, Jesus was saying that He was going to become the true Passover Lamb, and that when He went to the cross and His blood was shed for our sins, He would be making a way for us to worship God in our spirit and through the truth of His living Word.

Remember, we are spirit, and when we accept Christ as our Lord and Savior, we are filled with His Holy Spirit. We don't have to go to the mountain or to the temple in order to worship Him. We don't have to worship Him only at church, and we don't even have to sing worship songs to be worshiping Him (although these are important things to do regularly). No matter where we are, we take God with us because when we are born again we become the tabernacle of the Holy Spirit—He lives within us.

In the Old Testament, the tabernacle was only a place of visitation by God, but now He doesn't just visit us—we are His place of habitation. So everywhere we go, we can worship God in Spirit.

Jesus also mentioned worshiping in truth. We can worship Him in the truth of the Word if the Word abides in us, which it does when we read it and meditate on it every day (John 15:7).

Tonilee and I like the way Adam Clarke explains worshiping in spirit and truth in his Bible commentary: "[God] is an infinite Spirit… and can delight in those only who are made partakers of his own Divine nature. As all creatures were made by him, so all owe him obedience and reverence; but, to be acceptable to this infinite Spirit, the worship must be of a spiritual nature—must spring from the heart, through the influence of the Holy Ghost: and it must be in Truth, not only in sincerity. A man worships God in spirit, when, under the influence of the Holy Ghost, he brings all his affections, appetites, and desires to the throne of God; and he worships him in truth, when every purpose and passion of his heart, and when every act of his religious worship, is guided and regulated by the Word of God."[2]

WORSHIP MUST BE OF A SPIRITUAL NATURE— MUST SPRING FROM THE HEART.

Later, after Jesus told the woman at the well about this kind of worship, He was praying to the Father, and He said, *"Sanctify them by Your truth. Your word is truth"* (John 17:17). The meaning of *sanctify* is "to set apart to a sacred purpose"[3] or "to separate from profane things and dedicate to God."[4] We are set apart or made separate from the world because we have His Holy Word and His Holy Spirit, so we don't need to go looking for God anywhere, and we have no excuse to worship somebody else or to fall into worshiping false idols or false beliefs instead of worshiping the Lord.

What is true worship, then? It's offering our whole lives (or our bodies, as Paul said earlier) as a living sacrifice to the Lord. Having God's truth (His Word) and His Spirit inside of us is the only way we can offer ourselves like that, and it is the only way we can worship in Spirit and in truth. In a moment we're going to find out how we live as a sacrifice, but first let's see how the sacrifice of worship becomes holy and acceptable.

TRUE WORSHIP IS OFFERING OUR WHOLE LIVES AS A LIVING SACRIFICE TO THE LORD.

PLEASING WORSHIP

I was ministering to a group of people one time, and the question came up, "Why did all those animals have to die in the Old Testament? Why was the shedding of their blood the only way the people's sins could be forgiven?" The writer of Hebrews tells us that they were a shadow of good things in the future—a rough draft of what was to come through the shed blood of Jesus for our sins.

> *The law is only a shadow of the good things that are coming—not the realities themselves. For this reason it can never, by the same sacrifices repeated endlessly year after year, make perfect those who draw near to worship. If it could, would they not have stopped being offered? For the worshipers would have been cleansed once for all, and would no longer have felt guilty for their sins. But those sacrifices are an annual reminder of sins, because it is impossible for the blood of bulls and goats to take away sins.*
> —Hebrews 10:1-4 NIV

After Jesus' death, burial, and resurrection, there was no more need to kill one more animal as a sacrifice for sin. When Jesus shed His blood and died on the cross, all that was done away with. Now the minute we become born again, we are washed in the blood of Christ (spiritually speaking); there is no more need to sacrifice animals for the atonement of sin. Through Jesus' sacrifice on the cross, that has been done away with, once and for all.

WE MUST BE CAREFUL NOT TO GET CAUGHT UP IN THE SACRIFICE WE GIVE SO IT DOESN'T BECOME ALL ABOUT US AND WHAT WE'RE DOING.

If you are in Christ—if you know that Jesus died on the cross and His blood was shed for you and you are covered in that blood (spiritually speaking)[5] and you've accepted Him into your heart, and you know Him intimately—you are going to spend eternity in heaven, as your spirit will live on with Him forever when your body dies. And the Bible says that you will get a new body too (1 Corinthians 15:51-53). What more reasons do we need to worship the Lord than these?

The point is that the only way our sacrifice (or giving our lives to God and glorifying Him in everything we do) becomes holy and acceptable to the Lord is to have Christ in our hearts so when God looks upon us, He sees us through the blood of Jesus. Then God accepts and is pleased by whatever we are doing throughout our day that is in line with His Word. We just need to make sure that we are doing it as unto Him and from our heart of worship.

We must be careful not to get caught up in the sacrifice we give so it doesn't become all about us and what we're doing, because we can turn everything around to somehow please ourselves. I believe that Paul gave us the big picture of worship when he talked about making our lives and our bodies a living sacrifice to God. This simply means that in everything we do, we can step back and say, "Lord, I just want to worship You in this."

Sometimes worship in its simplest form is just being grateful. Isn't it great when we do something for someone else, and they say to us, "Thank you; I really appreciate you"? Tonilee and I are so blessed when we hear from people who tell us they appreciate what we're doing, regarding our ministry. It's not about giving in any other way, but just speaking a word of thanks and appreciation, so we know they are saying it from their heart and that they really mean it. That's all God wants too.

One time my (Bobbye) family came out to visit with me, and I love my sisters and my mom, but I got caught up in running around with them and doing many activities to make sure they had a good time. In the past, I used to worship those activities with them in the sense that my whole focus was on them and not God. But this time, even though I enjoyed the week we spent together, I made sure that I stepped back from time to time and worshiped the Lord, telling Him things like, "Lord, I'm so thankful that I have this family. I'm so thankful and grateful that I can be with them during this time." I love them, but I kept my focus on God.

Practicing worship is the best way to keep our focus on the Lord. We may be struggling in our marriage or with our children, or we may have a job-related challenge, but no matter what is going on, we can still say, "Lord, I just love You. I thank You and I'm grateful for where I am in my life because You have me here right now for Your plan and purpose, and You never leave me or forsake me." This is about loving the Lord with all of our heart, no matter what situation we may be facing.

PRACTICING WORSHIP IS THE BEST WAY TO KEEP OUR FOCUS ON THE LORD.

The problem is that we are in a physical body and so often, as Paul was saying, we tend to consider it a sacrifice to present our whole life to God in this way because we're afraid to lay down everything.

The last thing we want to do is to lay down what we consider to be important to us—perhaps it's our money or our career or what we feel is our own identity. The truth is that we wouldn't hesitate to do it if we understood that the blessings God gives us in return are so much more than anything we could ever think about laying down for Him.

If God should ask you to lay down something that is important to you, it isn't to punish you in some way. He may have something better for your good if you're willing to let go of what you have and trust Him with your life. Many times it's just a matter of God wanting to see where our heart of worship is for Him.

YOU CAN NEVER FULLY EXPERIENCE THE PRESENCE OF GOD IF YOU DO NOT UNDERSTAND AND EXPERIENCE TRUE WORSHIP.

We know that practicing the presence of worship may be a big concept to grasp, but we want you to look at worship in a new way. Maybe you haven't understood what worship is all about or maybe you just haven't made worship much of a priority because you weren't sure it's that important. We personally have learned over the years that it is step one to being in God's presence.

You can never fully experience the presence of God if you do not understand and experience true worship.

Where is your heart of worship? Are you at a place in your life where you are always caught up in all kinds of activities you think you should be doing, or do you just want to worship and be thankful to God no matter where you are or what's going on?

In Psalm 51:16 David said the Lord doesn't desire burnt offerings and animal sacrifices from us, but all He's really looking for is a broken heart and a contrite spirit. *The Message Bible* describes it this way.

> *Going through the motions doesn't please [God],*
> *a flawless performance is nothing to [God].*
> *I learned God-worship*
> *when my pride was shattered.*

*Heart-shattered lives ready for love
don't for a moment escape God's notice.*
—Psalm 51:16-17 MSG

Practicing the presence of worship brings our heart to the place where the only thing we can do is pray, "Lord, let my life be an offering to You." It helps to create a place in our heart that is so broken that we want nothing else but to offer all that we have and all that we are to God. Paul called it our reasonable service. I (Bobbye) believe that's when God says, "I've got some work for you to do now."

SERVICE AS WORSHIP

Present your bodies a living sacrifice, holy, acceptable to God, which is your reasonable service.
—Romans 12:1

The original Greek word for *service* in this verse is actually derived from the Greek word for *worship*.[6] What Paul was saying here is that when we are willing to present our bodies, or our lives, to God as a living sacrifice, we are actually giving ourselves over to a life of worship.

SOMETIMES CHRISTIANS CAN GET REALLY GOOD AT SPIRITUAL ACTING.

If you look at some other Bible translations of Romans 12:1, you'll find an interesting play on words used for "your reasonable service." The *New American Standard Bible* calls it *your spiritual service of worship*, and the *New International Version* Bible calls it *your spiritual act of worship*. Sometimes Christians can get really good at spiritual acting. You may laugh at that, but it all goes back to the heart. Is our reasonable service to the Lord coming from our heart or is it only an outward display?

Many Christians get involved in serving the Lord because we love Him and we want to serve Him. When we start to see God work in our lives and we come to the place where we are walking with the Lord, our hearts overflow with the desire to serve Him in some way. We may get involved in church by volunteering to teach Sunday school or run the nursery or lead a Bible study group or anything else that we can do there all because we want to worship God. Our hearts are drawn to service for that reason.

Most times we go into these situations with the right heart, but here's what can happen if we're not careful. We can take our eyes off of worshiping God through it and find ourselves in a place of just doing

THE OTHER SIDE OF SPIRITUAL SERVICE OR ACTS OF WORSHIP GOES BEYOND THE CHURCH.

the work, and suddenly we start complaining about everything: "If so and so is teaching that class, my children aren't going to it," or "I don't understand why they don't help us; they know we're in here needing help," or "The church this and the people that." The next thing we know, we're caught up in the activities instead of being there to serve the Lord.

We may not realize that we've been caught up in all the activities or that our attention has been taken off of God and put on the church work or whatever else we're doing to serve Him. If this is the case, then our heart and passion will be in the works, and we'll be caught up in fighting and gossiping and complaining. We may not call it worship, but we'll actually be worshiping those works; we may even be worshiping our own needs.

Can you see how easy it is to get your focus turned around even in serving the body of Christ?

The other side of spiritual service or acts of worship goes beyond the church. It isn't just about serving in some spiritual way. It's about how we behave in our daily lives, like when we're at the grocery store.

Are you someone who is really impatient when standing in line? You start griping and complaining, "That line's shorter and I'm cutting in over there." Or have you ever been short-tempered with a cashier, saying, "Could you hurry up please? I'm on a tight schedule here." Is that worshiping God?

I (Bobbye) know there's nothing that tries my patience like a deli market at the grocery store. I've even been known to go to three or four grocery stores, thinking I can get faster service because I go to the deli part every week, and I always seem to end up waiting forever in line. One day I stood in the deli line for twenty minutes, and about the time I thought the lady ahead of me was done, she asked for something else. As I was standing there, I was thinking, *Oh, Lord, just give me patience.*

WORSHIP THE LORD IN SOME WAY THROUGH YOUR ACTIONS, YOUR ATTITUDE, AND THE WORDS YOU SPEAK TO OTHERS.

The truth is that when we find ourselves in those places, so often being a witness or worshiping God in our hearts is the farthest thing from our mind. But instead of complaining, we could be saying, "Lord, thank You that I can be standing at this deli right now. Thank You that I have the money to buy this food. Thank You for this food."

We want to challenge you to make sure that wherever you go, you see yourself as carrying God with you and the place as an opportunity for you to worship the Lord in some way through your actions, your attitude, and the words you speak to others. You may need to pray quite a bit when you're there, but God already knows any struggles you may be going through, and He can help you if you ask Him.

When you're able to react in this way, you're beginning to get the practice of worship into your mind.

CHANGING THE WAY YOU THINK

So far we have talked about the heart and looked at the big picture of how our lives and our bodies can be a sacrifice to God. Now we're going to narrow it down a little bit more.

> *Do not be conformed to this world, but be transformed by the renewing of your mind, that you may prove what is that good and acceptable and perfect will of God.*
>
> —Romans 12:2

Paul began Romans 12 by talking about changing our hearts. Now in verse 2 he is saying that it's time to change the way we think. Sometimes as Christians we believe that we're not conformed to the world or caught up in the worldly lifestyle, but are we? How much does the world really influence us?

THE WORLD IS EVERYTHING THAT'S AROUND US, AND IT CAN HAVE A STRONG INFLUENCE OVER OUR LIVES.

The world is everything that's around us, and it can have a strong influence over our lives to conform to its ways. To *conform* is simply to do what is accepted, conventional, or traditional. It is following the world's standards instead of God's.

How do we avoid conforming? Do not look like the world, act like the world, get caught up in the things of the world, or think like the world. If you are, be transformed by renewing your mind or the way you think. This can only happen when you have the Holy Spirit inside of you, and you are worshiping God in Spirit and in truth.

Worship is definitely a place that begins in your heart, but you cannot practice it without changing how you think. Your mind is that mental organ within you that tells you it's time to practice worship.

Your mind is what helps discipline you and how you think, so you must be serious about where your mind is and what you put in it.

We live in a world that is changing so fast and is filled with such rapid stimulation that we've become programmed for speed and for instant gratification. Tonilee and I are so accustomed to sending e-mails and getting an immediate response that when our cable goes down on the Internet, we literally get the shakes. The television advertisements are faster, brighter, bolder, and bigger. The newspapers cover everything they possibly can.

> YOU MUST BE SERIOUS ABOUT WHERE YOUR MIND IS AND WHAT YOU PUT IN IT.

We are made to believe that we must be multitasking a hundred tasks at a time and doing everything imaginable. We put our own value system against how much we can get done and how fast we can do it. Isn't that somehow being conformed to the world?

How we look, how we dress, what we drive all play into our thoughts and our behavior as well. Before you know it, we may be Christians, we may have Christ in our hearts, and we may come to church, but we have to fit God and church into our schedule. We say to God, "Oh, yes, thank You, Lord, but I've got to go. Did You hear that prayer, Lord? Did You see that sacrifice I gave You? I want to make sure that I get that one in," and we put the Lord in our rotation of all the other activities and duties we have going on. Is that real worship? Is that what God wants from our hearts?

As Christians we have the availability to truly be in the presence of holy, perfect, righteous God, Creator of all of heaven and earth. But we get so caught up in the minutia that we forget He's really in charge. It is by His grace that we wake up in the morning. It is by His mercy that we have everything we have. It is by His infinite, unlimited, unconditional love that He answers any of our prayers or that He would even look upon us in the first place.

No matter how good we think we are or how much we think we are on the right track, if we really look inside ourselves and are honest, we'll find that we're not even close yet. The problem is that when we have so much going on in our life, we miss out on what God has for us.

AN ATTITUDE OF WORSHIP

By the time you finish reading this chapter, we pray that you truly understand what it is to worship and that you are not going to get into God's presence without it. You can't just skip that whole part of your relationship with the Lord and expect to experience His presence intimately and personally. How can you have a relationship with someone and never be with them intimately, never have conversations with them, or hold their hand?

HOW CAN YOU HAVE A RELATIONSHIP WITH SOMEONE AND NEVER BE WITH THEM INTIMATELY?

You may be thinking, *God is Spirit. I can't touch Him like that. I can't feel Him touch me.* Yes, you can. Isaiah called it going to the throne room of God, and he described seeing the Lord seated on His throne, high and lifted up, and the train of His robe filled the temple with glory (Isaiah 6:1-5). You probably won't see those things when you come into God's presence, but you may feel what Isaiah felt. He was in the presence of the Lord in this passage, and the first thing he realized was that his lips were unclean. In other words, he was repentant.

You can feel the presence of God so strongly that you find yourself in a place of repentance, yet you can feel His loving warmth totally engulfing you. There's no way we can experience the fullness of God's love because our flesh bodies wouldn't be able to handle it. But as you let go in your heart and allow the Holy Spirit to bring you into God's presence, you are going to experience the feeling of His love for you.

Once you're in that place with God, you may feel in your spirit that He is putting His arms around you because He inhabits our praises (Psalm 22:3 KJV). In your heart you may hear Him call out your name or tell you that He loves you and that He has a wonderful plan and purpose for your life—but nothing else will matter to you except being with Him. The reason is that you've entered into His presence, and you've come there because your heart and mind are set on worship.

ONCE YOU'RE IN THAT PLACE WITH GOD, YOU MAY FEEL IN YOUR SPIRIT THAT HE IS PUTTING HIS ARMS AROUND YOU.

You can't have that kind of experience without worship, so here are some suggestions to help you to practice worship so you can come into His presence like this for yourself.

CHANGE THE COURSE OF YOUR DAY

When you get up in the morning, what do you do first? We're not talking about heading to the bathroom or having your morning coffee, but what's the next thing you do that gets your mind going? Do you turn on the television? Do you have to hear the weather or the traffic report or what's happening in the news? Perhaps you're a newspaper person. Maybe you go outside every morning and get your newspaper and think that's better than turning on the television because it's more selective. What is good in either one? Most of the headlines are bad, so the first thing you put in your mind is negative.

I (Bobbye) believe that the news can be a tool of Satan because it's addictive. There's nothing wrong with watching the news or reading it in the newspaper, unless it becomes a problem because you start worshiping it—you need to watch it or read it all the time, starting in the morning. If that's the first thing you have to do every day, it's the first thing going into your mind, and most of the news is bad.

Why not get up in the morning and turn on a praise song? If you don't want to do that, pick a praise song that you know and start singing it. Put that in your mind first. I'm not even saying to open the Word at that point, but if you want to read a scripture, read a worship Psalm, something that is praising God. Just take time first thing in the morning to put something of the Lord in your mind, because that's what will tend to stay with you the rest of the day and change the course of your day.

If Satan can get a claw into your mind as soon as you wake up, you're probably going to be battling him throughout the day. But if you begin your day with the Lord, your cares and concerns are now competing with praising Him. You'll be in a much stronger place to start the day.

Maybe you're thinking that you can both get the news and do your devotion in the morning. After you get the morning traffic report and hear all the other news, then you go

TAKE TIME FIRST THING IN THE MORNING TO PUT SOMETHING OF THE LORD IN YOUR MIND.

sit at the table, have your coffee and doughnut, and start to read a praise Psalm in your Bible. But as you begin to tell the Lord you love Him, you very likely will start to think about the story you just heard or read about in the news and suddenly your mind will be on that instead of on God. Do you see how competing thoughts are pulling your mind away from focusing on the Lord?

It's hard to have the kind of self-control to block out that news and focus totally on Him. Why not avoid the struggle and just choose to put your mind on praise and worship to God when you get up?

Let me back up even before that and encourage you to try this: When you go to bed at night, ask the Holy Spirit to wake you up the next morning with a praise song, and to help you, when you get out of bed, to pick up the Word and read it or to listen to a worship song. Know today that He wants to help you to make that your lifestyle.

It takes practice to make worship a lifestyle, and here's where the practice comes in. The scenario may go something like this. The first day you get up to worship you will probably tell yourself, *I'll do it tomorrow.* Then tomorrow you get up, and you may listen to a minute of a praise song and go turn on the news; but each day you get up and make the effort to try again. You may need to pray before you get up and before you go to bed for God to help you to do this, but as you practice it over and over every morning, your habits will soon begin to change.

IT TAKES PRACTICE TO MAKE WORSHIP A LIFESTYLE, AND HERE'S WHERE THE PRACTICE COMES IN.

STAYING ON COURSE

When you are driving in the car, what do you listen to—talk radio, secular music, the classical station? Christian radio is great to turn on, but it's even better if you take the time to put on some praise songs. Turn off the secular music and put those songs in your mind to help you stay on course during the day.

I (Bobbye) still enjoy going to movies and watching good programs on television, but it's hard to find shows that are clean so I am very selective. Are you willing to sacrifice being entertained to avoid putting the wrong thoughts in your mind? When you watch ungodly and unclean entertainment, it's like a video of them keeps playing over and over in your mind and you can't stop it. You keep seeing the images you watched on the movie or television screen or on your computer. That's why pornography and other sexual issues are such a problem in our society.

When we watch them on the screen, those images keep playing over and over in our minds because they are really the grip of Satan on our thoughts. The only way to keep that from happening to us is to choose not to watch them and keep them out of our heads. It may seem like a sacrifice, but do you really want that junk in your mind?

Do whatever it takes to remind yourself to practice these things. Stick notes around your house and in your car, if necessary. Little by little you'll find that you are starting to cut out certain entertainment and activities that put your mind in places that take you from God. He has so much more for you than what the world has to offer.

If you are saved and you believe in Jesus Christ, Satan can't take away your salvation. He can't take your spirit when your physical body dies. But he can do many things that take away what God has for you on this earth. We mentioned before the struggle with the flesh. The desires of your flesh can draw you to the wrong forms of entertainment. If you are dealing with this kind of struggle, we encourage you to choose wisely and to put what we've been sharing with you into practice. Every step of the way, ask the Lord to help you—and be sure to tell Him that you love Him.

SATAN CAN'T TAKE YOUR SPIRIT WHEN YOUR BODY DIES. BUT HE CAN DO THINGS THAT TAKE AWAY WHAT GOD HAS FOR YOU ON THIS EARTH.

When was the last time you said, "I love You, Lord," either in your heart, in your mind, or with your lips and your voice? How many times a day do you say, "Thank You, Lord. I so appreciate that, Lord. Oh, Lord, You're so good"? Occasionally we may feel a little spiritual, and we may have a special moment with the Lord, like when we're sitting on the beach and we say, "What a beautiful sunset, Lord." That's fine, but I'm talking about thanking Him for His blessings all day, every day, in bad times as well as good ones.

How often do you say, "Thank You, Lord," when you're stuck in traffic? If you will begin to practice the principles in this book, they will turn into habits that become a part of you, and then bad situations like sitting in traffic won't seem so bad anymore. You'll be able to spend time with the Lord, worshiping Him, while you're in a long line at the grocery store or sitting in traffic or doing anything else that would normally upset you. All of a sudden, bad situations will seem to just disappear because you will be focused on God, not the circumstances. Try it and see what happens.

God wants you to have this kind of attitude in your heart because that's what He's going to bless.

PRACTICING THE PRESENCE OF WORSHIP

Before we close this chapter, we want to go a little deeper in this place of worship and share one more step: have uninterrupted quiet time with the Lord. You can worship God anywhere at anytime, but to really experience His presence, you need to be alone with Him in a place that's quiet. If you haven't done that, we encourage you to make it a priority.

Maybe you're thinking, *My days are so busy, you can't even imagine. There's no way I can have quiet time with God. I'm doing good just to talk to Him in the car in between phone calls.* We encourage you to pray about it and ask the Lord to give you time, even if it's only five or ten minutes at first.

That's why I (Bobbye) suggested getting alone with God early in the morning. Tonilee and I agree that it's the best time because it's quiet, and usually you can be alone. It may be a sacrifice. You may have to get up a little earlier, but if your heart's desire truly is to be in God's presence, it's worth the effort because this is the most incredible place to be. Keep in mind that as you practice this, it will become easier every day.

YOU CAN WORSHIP GOD ANYWHERE AT ANYTIME, BUT TO REALLY EXPERIENCE HIS PRESENCE, YOU NEED TO BE ALONE WITH HIM.

Say you've set aside ten minutes and you have your time and your place. Maybe it's at the beach sitting in your car or out in the countryside in a beautiful, wooded area. Perhaps it's outside on your porch or in a spare bedroom. Just be sure to turn your cell phone off and get away from your house phone, the television, and the noise, because the moment you commit to this quiet time, Satan will do everything imaginable to come after you to distract you. The phone will probably ring at least ten times, or you will suddenly remember a whole list of things you need to do right away.

You need to be alone with God and have no distractions.

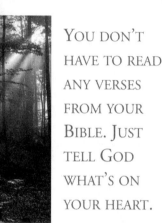

YOU DON'T HAVE TO READ ANY VERSES FROM YOUR BIBLE. JUST TELL GOD WHAT'S ON YOUR HEART.

Now that you have your quiet time and place, you may not be sure what to do next. First, take a deep breath and relax because your mind is probably going to be racing, thinking about all that you need to take care of today. Sit still; don't think, don't talk, don't try to work something out in your mind—just be quiet. As you're in that quiet place and you're relaxing, start talking to God. This is not the time to pray your list of wants and needs, but say something like, "Lord, I love You. You're so wonderful," and just start praising Him out loud.

You don't have to read any verses from your Bible. Just tell God what's on your heart. Thank Him for your life, your home, your family, the beautiful city you live in, and whatever else you can think of. Imagine yourself sitting at the feet of Jesus like Mary did when He visited her home (Luke 10:39), and start talking to Him with no expectation of Him talking back; it's just your worship to Him. Simply start from the wellspring of your heart and let your feelings for Him flow. He knows all about you anyway. He just wants to be in the center of your emotions and your life.

If you practice this in some way every day, you'll find that your mind will be trained and renewed and focused on God in a whole different way. There's really nothing you can give back to Him that even compares with His love for you, but you can still worship Him with all your heart and thank Him for all He's done for you.

Remember, a heart of worship longs to spend time with the Lord and desires to meditate on God's words. A heart of worship is sensitive to the Spirit as it quickly repents and is willing to yield to the ways of God. This kind of heart does not come naturally. It takes practice, but if we desire to be in His presence, it is absolutely necessary.

Tonilee and I have given you a different picture of worship from the usual view because worship isn't just singing a song in church. Your whole life is meant to worship God, and you can play that out in your daily activities and everything you do from morning all the way to the end of the day. We hope that you will make a commitment to practice the presence of worship and make it part of your life and make it a priority. Once you experience coming into God's presence through worship, there's no other place you will want to be.

BUILDING BLOCKS
■■■■■■■■■

■ Question 1: Look up Genesis 22:1-18.
  a. How did Abraham express worship in what he was willing to do with his only son? Explain in your own words.
  b. How did God respond to Abraham's obedience?

■ Question 2: Genesis 22:5 is the first time that the word *worship* is used in the Bible. Note that it is used in accordance with a sacrifice of such magnitude.
  a. What other example of sacrifice does this story remind you of?

b. How does that ultimate sacrifice bring us to a place of worship?

c. How does the act of sacrifice in our own lives apply to our act of worship? Explain.

■ Question 3: In what ways do you worship other gods?

■ Question 4: How do you practice worship in your personal life? Name some ways you spend time worshiping the Lord.

■ Question 5: Jesus told the woman at the well how to worship. From John 4:19-24.
a. How are we to worship the Lord?

b. What does this mean to you?

■ Question 6: We were created for worship and we will spend eternity worshiping the Lord. The book of Revelation gives us a glimpse of this type of worship. What does Revelation 4:8-11 say worship is like in heaven?

Chapter 6

HEART-TO-HEART TALKS WITH THE FATHER

Practicing the Presence of Prayer

H OW AWESOME TO EXPERIENCE VICTORY IN OUR lives! Yet many Christians face the agony of defeat more than the thrill of victory. Often the reason is closely linked to prayer. When you have a weak prayer life, your heart, soul, strength, and mind are not in tune with God's will—which means that His ways are not being accomplished in your life. To find intimacy in God's presence, you must know how to maintain a state of prayer as well as worship. So we're going to be looking at prayer in this chapter because it's prayer that brings you the power you need to live a victorious Christian life and embrace all the desires God has for you.

One Greek translation for the word *victory* is "nike"[1] and implies a conquest or means of success. For many people, *Nike* refers to the mega sporting enterprise that sells shoes and clothing. The products of that company are promoted by rich and successful athletes giving hope to those who at least want to look good even if they are not as talented or as victorious. The trouble with this concept of victory is that it tends to be skewed by what society respects—extraordinary achievements. Jesus gave us a different view of victory.

> *Whatever is born of God overcomes the world. And this is the victory that has overcome the world—our faith.*
>
> —1 John 5:4

Jesus came to tell us to just have faith, for through faith we can have the victory, but how many of us have victory in our lives today? Far too often, we face the agony of defeat. Jesus did not come to earth, give His life, and leave us His Holy Spirit, just so we could enter heaven. Yes, He came to give us eternal life when we believe in Him, but He wants us to experience heaven on earth every day of our lives.

FAITH, PRAYER, AND VICTORY ARE ALL INTERRELATED.

Heaven on earth in this day and age? Is such a goal really possible? The Bible says it is.

If you have accepted Jesus as your Savior, then you have been born of God and are His child. To even accept Jesus indicates a position of faith on your part, *For by grace you have been saved through faith…* (Ephesians 2:8). But real victory does not stop here; it begins here. Faith, prayer, and victory are all interrelated. Faith must be grown, matured, and developed; that is mainly done by the trials and tests of life. When we're in trouble, we're going to pray, and faith is increased every time we see God answer our prayers. This is one of the reasons prayer is so important for us.

Those of us who pray have victory simply because of our faith.

Keeping in mind that victory in Jesus is not defined the same way as victory in the world, how do you answer this question: *Does your life reflect more victories or more defeats?* If you've been experiencing one defeat after another, have you checked your prayer life lately? If you are not practicing prayer every day, you can most likely track your defeats to the moment that decision was made.

You may be thinking, *I want to pray more, but I don't know how to pray.* We'll be looking at several types of prayer and ways to pray because the goal of this chapter is to help you to learn how to pray effectively and fervently so that you will never stop praying. As with other challenges in our daily lives, we must practice prayer to see it work effectively, but developing the habit of prayer should be easier to do when you realize that taking time to pray is an absolute requirement in knowing the Lord and receiving His blessings.

WE MUST PRACTICE PRAYER TO SEE IT WORK EFFECTIVELY.

When I (Tonilee) first came to Christ, I didn't really know how to pray. I was fourteen and my life changed right away because I had a new peace that I'd never known before. I wasn't into drugs or anything like that, but for the first time I really began to understand who God is, and I felt His peace immediately—and I didn't want to do anything to quench that peace. So I would read the Bible all the time and I would pray, but I didn't really understand the way to pray.

I had been raised in a very formal, traditional church that would tell me what to say when I prayed. It was just a vain repetition over and over, so I never had a relationship in prayer with the Lord, except to pray those "911" types of prayers—"Lord, help me!"—because they just come out of the wellspring of our hearts.

As I was growing in my walk with the Lord, I went to a large secular high school. I really had a desire to have a Christian friend, so I talked to my mom about it and we decided to start a Bible study in our home. I didn't know who to invite because none of my friends were Christians, and I didn't know the Christian kids who were in that school. My mom and I were hoping that our Bible study would grow into something big, but at first it looked as though it was just going to be the two of us.

One day a girl who sat behind me in one of my classes told me that the day before two people had come to her house to talk about God with her family. That prompted me to pray a quick prayer in my head, *God, I'll ask her to come to my Bible study. Show me if that's Your will.* So I turned around and invited her, and to my surprise she said yes. That night at our Bible study, she accepted Christ as her Savior, and when we were driving her home from our house, I realized that God put that desire in my heart to invite her in the first place, and then He gave me the power to accomplish it.

It seemed so easy to pray and have someone come to Christ that I figured something must be wrong. So I asked God to show me how to pray to get my prayers answered like that all the time. Soon in my Bible reading I came across a Scripture passage in Luke 11 that I was familiar with from church. It told how the disciples said the same thing to Jesus that I had said, *"Lord, teach us to pray..."* (v.1), and He did.

> He [Jesus] *said to them, "When you pray, say:*
> *Our Father in heaven,*
> *Hallowed be Your name.*
> *Your Kingdom come.*
> *Your will be done*
> *On earth as it is in heaven.*
> —Luke 11:2

When Jesus came to earth, the kingdom of God came through Him. As Christians, we are supposed to follow His example, so when

I read that verse, I realized that God's kingdom could come through me too because I'm on earth. But I wanted more proof that this was true and that God wanted it for me.

A little later on, I came across a verse in which the Pharisees asked Jesus when the kingdom of God was going to come.

He [Jesus] *answered them and said, "The kingdom of God does not come with observation."*

—Luke 17:20

In other words, they were not going to see it coming.

"Nor will they say, 'See here!' or 'See there!' For indeed, the kingdom of God is within you."

—Luke 17:21

I'm born again and filled with the Holy Spirit, and this verse reinforced that I have what it takes to let the kingdom of God flow from within me right here on earth, and since God said that and promised it to us in this Scripture, I decided to claim that promise for myself and started praying that verse over my life. Soon I began to pray other verses in the Bible as well because I believed that it is God's will to speak His Word in our prayers and that He will take care of whatever we pray.

During one of my quiet times with the Lord, I found another Bible verse to pray that says that the heart's desire of Jesus is to seek and to save the lost (Luke 19:10). I began to pray that verse along with my request for people I came in contact with to come to Christ. The Lord answered my prayers and soon I was leading people to Jesus on airplanes. Patients in a hospital I worked at were coming to Christ—it just seemed that whenever He put someone on my heart to pray for and witness to, I did it and they accepted Jesus as their Lord and Savior.

During that time I thought I had learned everything there was to know about prayer, but it was just the tip of the iceberg.

Some of the people I led to the Lord received the gift of speaking in tongues, and one day I told God that I wanted that gift too. I was stunned to hear Him impress on my heart, *Why do you want to pray in another language when you haven't learned to pray in English yet?* He wasn't saying that I couldn't have the gift of tongues but that there's more to prayer than the way I was praying.

I used to think of prayer as singularly focused on the things I was asking for, but prayer involves so much more than just our requests. In this chapter I want to take you to the next step of intimacy with God and help you to find the place of continual communication—or prayer—with Him. So I'm going to share with you what I have learned about true prayer and what it means to practice the presence of prayer every day.

> PRAYER INVOLVES SO MUCH MORE THAN JUST OUR REQUESTS.

Bobbye showed you how you can practice the presence of God by worshiping Him in every situation. Humbly coming to the Lord in prayer is another way of including Him in every aspect of our lives. That is easy to do when we realize that God cares about everything we care about (1 Peter 5:6-7).

COMMUNICATING WITH GOD

After Jesus' death on the cross and His burial, He arose from the grave. On the day of His resurrection He said to Mary Magdalene, *"Do not cling to Me, for I have not yet ascended to My Father* [in His throne room in heaven]; *but go to My brethren and say to them, 'I am ascending to My Father and your Father, and to My God and your God'"* (John 20:17). What did Jesus mean? It is only because of Him that our prayers have access to and reach the throne room of God. The significance of this is described in Mark 15:37-38, *And Jesus cried out with a loud voice, and breathed His last. Then the veil of the temple* [The Most Holy Place] *was torn in two from top to bottom.*

The Most Holy Place or the Holy of Holies is considered to be a type of heaven, "and the tearing of the veil to signify that the way to heaven was now open to all."[2] Before this, only the priests could enter into the Holy of Holies—a lay person was not allowed to go beyond the veil. The point is that Jesus' sacrifice, being the perfect sin offering for us, allows us to have a personal relationship with the God of all creation. Every relationship takes time and attention, and our relationship with the Lord is no different.

EVERY RELATIONSHIP TAKES TIME AND ATTENTION, AND OUR RELATIONSHIP WITH THE LORD IS NO DIFFERENT.

We saw earlier that God is a Spirit, and each of us is spirit, so we have a God-given internal desire to communicate with Him. No relationship can exist without some form of communication, and our primary form of communication with God is through an act of prayer. Simply stated, prayer is our conversation, or way of communicating, with the Lord. In its most basic state, to pray is just talking to God, but the ways in which we "talk" can take on very different forms and methods, as we see in these three major forms of prayer.

1. *Petitions*—Presenting your requests or desires to God, and praying for your needs and wants.

2. *Intercessions*—Making requests on behalf of others, and praying for others.

3. *Supplications*—Asking God to grant a solution for a specific situation, as Daniel did when he prayed about the nation of Israel deviating from God's plan and path for their lives. (See Daniel 9.)

God has given us a broad range of prayers we can pray for ourselves and others that empower us to live above our circumstances, including (1) prayers of praise; (2) prayers of protection; and (3) prayers of peace. These prayers bring power to us because they lead us to pray in accordance with God's will instead of our own desires.

God honored the prayers of men and women in the Bible, and they are examples for us to follow. Biblical prayers include the confession of sin, praise in acknowledging God's character and ability to answer, and as we just saw, supplications of asking for specific requests (for oneself, petition; for others, intercession). But the key is praying from your heart in all sincerity based on and agreeing with His truth.

> REGARDLESS OF WHAT KIND OF PRAYERS YOU PRAY, YOU CAN HAVE CONFIDENCE THAT GOD HEARS.

Just as worship is to come from our heart and mouth, our prayers should also be from our heart and come forth from our mouth. The fact is, the Lord knows what we want and what we need before we ever tell Him, but He is more concerned with the honesty and sincerity of how we speak to Him.

Regardless of what kind of prayers you pray, you can have confidence that God hears your prayers and will answer them. He may not answer in your timing or do what you expect, but He will answer in a way and time that's best for you.

> *"Call to Me, and I will answer you, and show you great and mighty things, which you do not know."*
> —Jeremiah 33:3

It is evident from this verse alone that God wants us to pray and that He wants to answer us to bless us. In my (Tonilee) quest to learn how to pray, it became very clear to me from this verse and others that I came across that God wants to give to us, but He won't give without being asked. I learned that He'll answer whatever I pray about (when it is in line with His Word) in ways that bring Him all the glory (John

14:13)—answers that we could never make happen on our own—so that our hearts stay centered on Him and not on ourselves.

Jesus died for you so that He may be included in your life for Him. Sometimes He will even allow you to go through situations and circumstances that force you to pray for His will to be done. The reason is that He wants to get the glory for miracles that occur through you because of His work. So whatever you pray about allows Him to use you for His glory.

God has given you everything in life and godliness to be successful in the things of God (2 Peter 1:3). He has withheld nothing from you—but it is your choice. We've seen that we are temples of the Holy Spirit (when we are born again). Instead of a temple (or tabernacle) in which to worship and pray as the Israelites had, we have *become* His temple, or His *house of prayer* (Isaiah 56:7). Our bodies are called to be a living, breathing house whose interior is designed to be painted and carpeted with prayer. But the responsibility to pray is on you. God will not make you include Him.

WHEN YOU DON'T PRAY, YOU DENY GOD THE OPPORTUNITY TO DO A MIRACLE FOR YOU.

You need to get a revelation that wherever you are and whatever you go through, God is there also, and He wants to be included. Psalm 118:15 KJV talks about prayers coming from *the tabernacles of the righteous* (those who believe) and implies that the Lord does mighty things for us when we pray. Think about it: When you don't pray, you deny God the opportunity to do a miracle for you.

When I realized that, I decided that I was going to pray about everything. I didn't let anything cross my path without praying about it because I wanted to see the Lord move in my life with such power that people would know that this girl's different. Actually every believer should pray that we never make decisions without God so that His ways and His will can be accomplished in our lives.

Are you getting the big picture of why we need to pray? If those reasons don't make you want to pray more, this one should: The Bible tells us to *pray without ceasing* (1 Thessalonians 5:17), and to pray always (Luke 18:1) because prayer wins battles.

PUTTING ON YOUR ARMOR

Do you ever feel as though you are in the midst of a battle where the odds are stacked against you? Or maybe you see the giants, hear their taunts, and decide to hide out, as opposed to standing up to them like David did with Goliath in 1 Samuel 17. The truth is, we are all in a spiritual battle and there is one clear Enemy.

> *Finally, my brethren, be strong in the Lord and in the power of His might. Put on the whole armor of God, that you may be able to stand against the wiles of the devil. For we do not wrestle against flesh and blood, but against principalities, against powers, against the rulers of the darkness of this age, against spiritual hosts of wickedness in the heavenly places. Therefore take up the whole armor of God, that you may be able to withstand in the evil day, and having done all, to stand. Stand therefore.*
> —Ephesians 6:10-14

Paul is very clear here on who we're fighting against. We might think all of our problems have to do with our husband or our children or some other person, but that's not the case. According to Paul, we aren't struggling or wrestling against flesh at all, but against principalities, powers, rulers of the darkness of this age, against spiritual hosts of wickedness—all of these fall under the Enemy's domain.

Yet Paul tells us that we are to stand against the wiles of the devil. In other words, we are to plant our feet so firmly that when the devil comes after us, we're able to say, "I'm not moving." The only way you can plant your feet that firmly on the ground when you are under attack is by finding that spiritual place on your knees—that place of prayer—whether you physically kneel down or your heart kneels.

Praying always with all prayer and supplication in the Spirit, being watchful to this end with all perseverance and supplication for all the saints.

—Ephesians 6:18

IT IS ON OUR KNEES THAT WE LEARN TO FIGHT SPIRITUALLY.

The strongest weapon we can have is a tender heart that knows how to turn to the Lord on our knees and pray. It is on our knees that we learn to fight spiritually. It is on our knees that we are able to take every thought captive.

Though we walk in the flesh, we do not war according to [against] the flesh. For the weapons of our warfare are not carnal but mighty in God for pulling down strongholds, casting down arguments and every high thing that exalts itself against the knowledge of God, bringing every thought into captivity to the obedience of Christ.

—2 Corinthians 10:3-5

In another verse, the Lord tells us through Peter that the devil is roaming around like a lion seeking someone to devour. (See 1 Peter 5:8.) If you appear to be a likely candidate who's not standing firm in the things of God and controlling your thoughts, you will be his next supper—and that's a bad place to be.

Make no mistake about it. Satan will use whatever tactics he can to get to us in order to frighten us and to keep us from fighting back. He will play tricks on our minds so that we see giants that are not real. He will frustrate our plans so he can get the peace within our heart to crush into a flesh frenzy. He will deceive us into believing that we have no ability to win.

The good news is that God has not left us defenseless. Ephesians 6 describes several spiritual weapons Paul calls the armor of God that are available to all of us who are born again and are actively pursuing our walk with the Lord.

THE GOOD NEWS IS THAT GOD HAS NOT LEFT US DEFENSELESS.

Truth, righteousness, peace, faith, and salvation are more than words. Learn how to apply them. You'll need them throughout your life.
—Ephesians 6:14-17 MSG

So many Christians are apathetic and complacent to the wiles of Satan. They live on the defense instead of moving forward with God on the offense. It's true that the Enemy won't bother them because that's just where he wants them to be, but God has so much more for them—and us. The Lord has won the battle; we just have to put the armor on.

I (Tonilee) learned early in my Christian life that we *apply* or put on the armor of God by praying the armor, but wouldn't it be so much easier if we could just physically put it on? If we could just wake up every morning and say, "I'm going to put on that breastplate now; okay, now I've got my helmet on too," and then literally put on the rest of the armor? We'd have no problem remembering that we were wearing it. But it didn't take long for me to learn, as I kept growing in and seeking the Lord, that it doesn't come this easily.

Several years ago when I was first starting to teach the Bible in a group setting, I would be so nervous beforehand that I would just be shaking and I heard things in my mind like, "What do you think you're doing? Why are you getting up there to teach? What do you have to say to these people anyway? Do you want them to emulate you? And what if you stutter? What if you don't read the Bible passages right?" I was just tormented by all those "what-ifs."

It was a good thing I had six weeks to recuperate until the next class because it used to wipe me out completely. I would spend hours and hours trying to recover. Then finally one of the administrators of the class said to me, "Tonilee, you need to put on the armor of God."

I thought I had already put it on, but as I looked back over the torment I was going through before each class, I knew it wasn't true. I realized that if I didn't learn what it really meant to put on the armor of God to fight against the fear, I would not be able to continue teaching those Bible classes, regardless of where my heart was with the Lord.

That woman helped me by sitting me down right before I'd get up to teach a class and reading to me from Ephesians 6. As she did, I would imagine myself putting on each piece of the armor of God, which helped me tremendously.

It brought me the confidence that I needed to get up to speak in front of a group without shaking. I realized that putting on the armor through prayer protects your mind because your heart is already for the Lord. I was getting up there to teach because I knew that the Lord had called me to do that and my heart just wanted to be obedient, but my mind couldn't take captive the negative thoughts of fear. Praying the armor changed my focus from fear to God, and the Enemy couldn't harass me anymore.

PUTTING ON THE ARMOR THROUGH PRAYER PROTECTS YOUR MIND.

One of the most powerful tools the Enemy has against us is fear. Fear keeps us from facing the giants of troubles, challenges, and other concerns. Fear keeps us from ever achieving victory because we are afraid to enter the battle. Fear becomes our own trap of despair, depression, and disillusionment.

So often this battle takes place in our own minds with giants conjured up in our thoughts, but this is not God's will for us. If you can't take the negative thoughts captive, then you will be living a life of defeat instead of living a life of victory with the Lord. No battle is too great for God. That's why *prayer is essential in this ongoing warfare* (Ephesians 6:18 MSG).

MORE PIECES OF THE PUZZLE

You may be facing some kind of struggle right now, but I believe today can be your day of victory. This can be the day that you stop running, stop hiding, and stop believing the lies of Satan. Let's look at some more pieces of the puzzle that will help you to step out in faith, face the Enemy head on, and claim the victory that is yours.

THE WORD OF GOD

The question is often asked, "How do I pray in God's will?" Or, "How do I know if I am praying God's will?" The way to be certain that we are praying in accordance with God's will is to pray His Word back to Him.

MEDITATING ON (THINKING ABOUT OR PONDERING) THE WORD WORKS ON YOUR HEART AND CHANGES THE WAY YOU THINK.

To pray the Word of God, you need to know what it says. God's thoughts are contained in His Word, so the more you read it, the more you will learn about Him. Keeping His Word in your heart every day is important too because meditating on (thinking about or pondering) the Word works on your heart and changes the way you think. Remember, Satan's plan of attack hits your mind. He can't read your mind, but he can discern what you are thinking by your words and behavior.

That's why praying the Word is essential. I encourage you to begin by praying Ephesians 1:18—that the Lord opens your eyes and gives you discernment to understand the devil's strategies and how to use the God-given weapons to defeat him.

The writer of Hebrews describes the Word of God as a sword that divides your soul from your spirit. (See Hebrews 4:12.) We learned earlier that there's a great conflict that goes on between your soul (your mind, will, and emotions) and your spirit once you come to Christ. When you read the Word and meditate on it, the Word divides your soul from your spirit so you can tell the difference between what is coming from you or from the devil versus what is coming from God.

The Word clears up your motives and clarifies your intents and your thinking. Then when you pray back the Word, slowly your soul can come in line with the things of the Spirit, and that's how you live a life that's not double minded.

IN TIMES OF DECISION MAKING OR UNCERTAINTY, WE NEED TO ASK FOR WISDOM.

If we are the Lord's temple, then He dwells in us and wants to be included in all of our thoughts. Through the Word, you can take the thoughts captive that aren't from God. As you get into the Word, it can change you and give you the power to walk in victory. You can have power then to claim those verses back, knowing absolutely what the will of God is for your life. As your prayers are conformed to God's will (His Word), He can answer the desires of your heart.

The Bible gives us numerous examples of what and how to pray for every type of situation we encounter. For instance, in times of decision making or uncertainty, we need to ask for wisdom. We know that it is God's will for us to pray for wisdom because James 1:5 tells us to ask for wisdom and that God will give it without restraint.

Let's look at a specific example of how to pray the Word and apply it to your life.

"For My thoughts are not your thoughts,
Nor are your ways My ways,"
says the LORD.
"For as the heavens are higher than the earth,
So are My ways higher than your ways,
And My thoughts than your thoughts."
—Isaiah 55:8-9

After reading this passage, one example of praying these verses could be praise and confession:

Dear Lord, I praise You that Your ways are higher than my ways and that Your thoughts are higher than my thoughts. How awesome that You know how high the heavens are from the earth! Forgive me, Father, for thinking I have any sort of control over my situations. Forgive me for not giving everything over to you and for thinking that my ways are better than Yours. Please help me to trust You today. Thank You for Your Word and for speaking to my heart. I trust You to take care of the heavens and the earth, and I trust You to take care of me too. In Jesus' name, amen.

WHEN WE LEARN TO PRAISE GOD THROUGH OUR TRIALS, WE ALSO FIND INTIMACY IN HIS PRESENCE.

The Word of God must be as integral a part of our daily lives as our prayers are. We often will pray when we find ourselves in trouble, since praying comes naturally during times of crisis, but without reading and seeking God's will in His Word, our prayers can be centered on our will instead of God's. It is also through God's Word that we find peace and comfort, knowing that our prayers are heard. It is when we learn to praise God through our trials that we also find intimacy in His presence. To practice His presence through prayer means that we must learn to apply His Word in our prayers every day.

THE NAME OF JESUS

When we become born again, Jesus gives us the authority or the power of attorney to use His name in prayer anytime and anyplace. It is the same principle as a woman who takes her husband's last name when she gets married and can use it wherever she goes and whatever she does. The dictionary defines *power of attorney* as someone who has been given the authority to act for or to represent another.[3] We represent Jesus just as a wife represents her husband. (See Isaiah 54:5.)

JESUS GIVES US THE AUTHORITY OR THE POWER OF ATTORNEY TO USE HIS NAME IN PRAYER ANYTIME AND ANYPLACE.

Jesus talked about using His name several times in the Bible. Once He told His disciples, *"Until now you have asked nothing in My name. Ask, and you will receive, that your joy may be full"* (John 16:24). Just before saying that, Jesus had told them, *"In that day you will ask Me nothing. Most assuredly, I say to you, whatever you ask the Father in My name He will give you"* (v. 23). Apparently praying in Jesus' name was a new concept to them.

The disciples hadn't asked anything in Jesus' name at that time because they physically had Him with them, so they didn't think about using His name in prayer. But look at what happened when they started speaking the name of Jesus among the people.

The Lord had sent the disciples out to several cities to witness and minister to others. They went representing Jesus as they preached and healed and cast out demons in His name. The Bible records that when they returned, they were rejoicing and told Jesus, *"Lord, even the demons are subject to us in Your name"* (Luke 10:17).

What happens when we pray in or speak the name of Jesus?

God also has highly exalted Him and given Him the name which is above every name, that at the name of Jesus every knee should bow, of those in heaven, and of those on earth, and of those under the earth, and that every tongue should confess that Jesus Christ is Lord, to the glory of God the Father.

—Philippians 2:9-11

Is it any wonder that the devil and his demons shudder at the mention of that name?

Jesus said in John 14:12-14, *"Most assuredly, I say to you, he who believes in Me…whatever you ask in My name, that I will do, that the Father may be glorified in the Son. If you ask anything in My name, I will do it."* It all goes back to the matter of the heart. We receive in His name by asking with His heart, but we can only understand His heart by knowing His Word and developing a relationship with Him through prayer.

THE ENEMY LOVES TO COME INTO OUR MINDS AND FILL US WITH GUILTY AND SELF-CONDEMNING THOUGHTS.

THE BLOOD OF JESUS

The Enemy loves to come into our minds and fill us with guilty and self-condemning thoughts about all the things that we've done wrong like, "You're not worthy to be a child of God. You did those sins after you knew Jesus. Are you still forgiven for that? Who do you think you are to be doing some service for God with the past that you have, one that you haven't even overcome yet?"

All those kinds of thoughts are not from the Lord. They're from the devil, and they can keep us out of God's awesome plan for our lives if we don't know that the blood of Christ covers us from all sins—from sins in the past, from sins that we are doing presently, and from any sin that we will do in the future.

Of course, I'm not talking about physical blood here but a powerful spiritual weapon to use against the wiles of the devil. (Remember, we're not dealing with a flesh-and-blood enemy, but with evil spiritual forces). We apply or are covered in the blood of Jesus the same way as the other spiritual weapons we've looked at—by speaking or pleading it over ourselves and our loved ones.

For instance, you can pray or speak the blood over your son or daughter, saying, "Lord, cover my child in Your blood as he goes to school today," or "Lord, forgive me for that sin; thank You that it's washed in Your blood and that You remember it no more" (1 John 1:7; Psalm 103:12).

Through Jesus' blood we have salvation, power, healing, deliverance, and protection from every attack of the Enemy. It's the blood that enables us to come boldly to the throne of God and say, "Lord, it's not by my righteousness that I'm coming to You, but it's because I'm covered in the blood that I can come to You and ask You anything that is in my heart."

> THROUGH JESUS' BLOOD WE HAVE SALVATION, POWER, HEALING, DELIVERANCE, AND PROTECTION FROM EVERY ATTACK OF THE ENEMY.

Satan doesn't want you to know about the blood of Jesus because the blood repels him and all his evil buddies. So if your sins have been preventing you from praying, you're believing the liar, who's been a murderer and a liar from the very beginning. The blood of Jesus cleanses you from all of that.

THE HOLY SPIRIT

John 15:16 was another piece of the puzzle God led me to when He was teaching me how to pray.

> [Jesus said,] *"You did not choose Me, but I chose you and appointed you that you should go and bear fruit, and that your*

fruit should remain, that whatever you ask the Father in My name He may give you."

We ask in prayer because God wants to give to us so that He can be glorified, but He wants us to bear fruit too, and the Holy Spirit is the One responsible for fruit in our lives. We looked at the Holy Spirit in an earlier chapter, but He plays an important part in our prayer life.

THE HOLY SPIRIT IS THE ONE RESPONSIBLE FOR FRUIT IN OUR LIVES.

Think about it: We pray to God the Father, we end our prayers in Jesus' name, and we're the one in the middle to fulfill God's will on earth as it is in heaven. The point is that the Holy Spirit is in the middle with us because God has given Him to us, which is the same thing as if Jesus were with us himself. The Holy Spirit lives inside of us and His role in the middle of our prayer life is two-fold: He puts desires on our heart that we can pray back to God, and He intercedes for us when we don't know how to pray.

A great verse in Romans 8 tells us that when we don't know what to pray, even our groaning counts because the Spirit knows what's inside our heart (v. 26). Corrie ten Boom was an author, evangelist, Holocaust survivor, and a powerful woman of God who understood the importance of prayer. She once said that the ultimate place of prayer is when you get to the point that you have no words because you're completely in the Spirit and you trust Him.

The Spirit of God is in us in the middle, bringing the Word we've read and heard back to our remembrance so we can pray His will in that place of pain, in that place of hurt, in that place of trial and temptation. He will provide a way of escape through our prayers as we're surrendering continually to Him because He is the One in the middle who is responsible for fruit—love, joy, peace, patience, kindness, goodness, faithfulness, gentleness and self-control (Galatians 5:22-23 NIV)—through the work of God in our life.

When I (Tonilee) read John 15:16 and realized that God can only work in our life through the Holy Spirit, I asked the Lord to teach me to pray about everything and in every place from the shopping mall to the hospital bed to the grocery store to the classroom so that I completely understood how to practice His presence through prayer.

When you get to the point that you start coming to the Lord first, telling Him what you want instead of talking to yourself trying to work things out or telling your husband or your children or your friends or your mother or your father, that's when you will start seeing the Lord work in your life and bring about miracles.

The story of King Hezekiah is a great illustration of the power of prayer. He was a king of Israel who brought God's people back to worshiping the Lord only. One time a strong nation threatened to defeat him, but he didn't surrender. Instead, he worked hard to prepare the city and the people for war, and encouraged them that the Lord would help them and fight their battles (2 Chronicles 32:7-8), and God did just that—*He took care of them on every side* (v. 22 NIV).

> THE STRONGEST WEAPON IS A TENDER HEART THAT KNOWS THE SCRIPTURES AND HOW TO TURN TO THE LORD ON OUR KNEES.

We worship a God who takes care of us on every side too. It was good that Hezekiah prepared for battle, but it was better that he prepared his heart to turn to the Lord. The arm of flesh is limited, which is why we need to be prepared to fight as we use the weapons God has given us. The strongest weapon is a tender heart that knows the Scriptures and how to turn to the Lord on our knees.

If you are in a situation today in which you need to see the Lord on your side, use the weapons He has given you, but be sure to go to your knees and start asking Him for help. He is waiting to show

His power no matter what the issue is you are facing. No battle is too great for the Lord.

COME BOLDLY IN PRAYER

NO BATTLE IS TOO GREAT FOR THE LORD.

Those were the last pieces of the puzzle that I put together in learning how to pray, and this is what I finally understood. The Lord wants His will done on earth as it is in heaven, and we're on earth to fulfill that. He's given us spiritual weapons, He's given us His Holy Spirit, He's given us His name, His Word, and the blood of Jesus, so anything we do that looks as if we're sinning, even to the point of no return, He covers completely when we confess it to Him. That means we can walk in freedom and still come to Him boldly in prayer.

Sometimes when God is training you how to pray, and your soul is warring against your spirit, you can get tired in the battle and feel like you don't know if you can do it anymore. So here are a few points to remember that will encourage you and help you to keep going.

Whatever desire you have on your heart, include the Lord in it.
Just make sure the first desire is always to love Jesus. You can start your prayer by saying something like, "Jesus, all I really want is You. I just want to see heaven open up on earth because You want to use me to do it, but, Lord, I also have these other desires that I'm asking You to fulfill."

Stop praying that same prayer when it becomes repetitious.
I'm talking about those prayers that you have in your heart that feel as though you're saying them over and over. It could be anything. It could be about your spouse or your weight or your children or the car you drive. Whatever it is, when you get to the point that you know you keep repeating the same prayer, just stop praying about

it. Say to the Lord, "I believe You hear my prayers and there's obviously a reason why this situation is still in my life, so please help me to acknowledge You in it. I'm laying this prayer on the altar and it is now Yours. Thank You for taking care of it for me." Then walk away in peace, and pray about other things, knowing that God will take care of this one for you too.

Relax.

This is especially important when you've been praying a Scripture you know is a promise from God for you and believe that God has you going down the path you're on because it's His will; then all of a sudden God tells you to turn right, when you are only a few steps away from having the very thing you thought He was going to give you. God may have had you pray those prayers just to get you to this place so that you'll take a new direction.

SOMETIMES IT'S OUR INTERPRETATION OF THE PROMISE THAT GETS US INTO TROUBLE.

If you're not careful, you can stumble at that point, wondering if you really heard from God in the first place. Most likely God did give you the promise, and He is true to His Word. Sometimes it's our interpretation of the promise that gets us into trouble. So be sure you continue to follow that path, but relax no matter where God leads you so that you will remain with Him through it all.

Set aside time to pray.

It takes time and trial and error to develop a prayer life so make time for it every day. You can wake up earlier in the morning, if necessary. If you need help remembering to pray throughout the day, you could buy a bracelet in a Christian bookstore that says PRAY on it. Or you could find your own way to remind yourself. When I have something

that I need to pray about for myself or if someone asks me to inter-
cede for them and I know it's going to slip my mind because it's a
busy day, I will wear my watch on the opposite wrist just to remind
me that I need to pray. If you need to, use little tricks like that to
remind yourself to stay in prayer, but basically just include the Lord
in all your thoughts and in all that you do.

Keep a Prayer Journal.

I could not get to the point of learning to pray without ceasing
without keeping a prayer journal. Bobbye and I are very strong advo-
cates for prayer journaling. We personally have learned over the years
that journaling our prayers brings much comfort and peace in both
good and bad times.

There is something special about writing out prayers. As we've
seen, having a regular quiet time spent in God's Word and in prayer
is the absolute requirement in knowing our Lord. Writing in a prayer
journal is another way to have intimate devotional time between
you and your heavenly Father. Bobbye and I encourage you to write
down and record your prayers and the answers you receive from God
for several reasons.

- To keep you accountable to pray
- To keep your mind focused
- To reveal your motives (James 4:3)
- To change your desires (Psalm 84:11)
- To seek God's face and His will (Matthew 6:33)
- To see what pleases God's heart (Psalm 37:4)
- To become dependent on Him alone (Proverbs 3:5-6)

Blessings can come from writing down your prayers. This habit
needs to be formed and maintained because of the good fruit it can
produce in your life. We tend to quickly forget what we read or hear,
but we remember what we write down and meditate over. And it's

always encouraging to go back and read the history of God's faithfulness in journals written at different times and stages of life. The Lord wants us always to remember; He tells us in His Word not to forget (Deuteronomy 4:9), and a prayer journal is an effective tool to help you remember God's goodness all the days of your life.

Remember that Jesus understands.

Have you ever poured your heart out to someone but felt worse afterwards because you knew that no matter how hard you tried to express your feelings, they just didn't understand? True understanding and sympathy can only come when the person with whom you are sharing a personal problem has lived through the same type of situation.

When I think of the sufferings that Christ endured here on earth, I am comforted that He understands my sufferings. No one was more rejected, ridiculed, misunderstood, and alone than Jesus. Even though He was fully God, He was also fully man. Jesus dealt with the same emotions and temptations in His flesh as we do, yet He overcame them to remain without sin. But Jesus never focused on His own pain; His concern and compassion was for the people. He knew and understood the pain

JESUS SAYS TO *COME BOLDLY TO THE THRONE OF GRACE...* (HEBREWS 4:16) WHERE YOU WILL FIND HELP IN TIME OF NEED.

Lazarus' sisters were feeling when Lazarus died (John 11), and He knows the pain that we feel. I try to remember these things in my weakest moments, and know that I am not alone.

Are you tired or hurting? Maybe you feel as though no one really understands or cares? Jesus says to *come boldly to the throne of grace...* (Hebrews 4:16) where you will find help in time of need and seize the mercy and grace that has been freely given by Him. His sufferings were for this very reason, so that we (you and I) can pour out our hearts in prayer to the One who truly understands and the only One who can truly save us.

PRAYER IS A CHOICE

Prayer is a choice as much as anything else we need to do to live in God's presence. We choose to receive Jesus into our hearts. We choose to spend quiet time with Him and to read His Word. And we choose whether or not to pray. It takes time, diligence, and determination to develop a prayer life that is powerful enough to move mountains and to part Red Seas, but nothing is as satisfying as knowing you have touched the heart of God when He answers your prayers.

PRAYER IS DESIGNED TO BE A TWO-WAY CONVERSATION.

It may surprise you to know that the goal of prayer is not just for us to do all of the talking. Prayer is designed to be a two-way conversation. That means the goal is for us to hear God talk back to us—we talk as well as listen to the Lord. God speaks through His Word, so when we pray with His Word, we will learn to recognize His voice. At that point, our prayers truly do bring us into His presence.

BUILDING BLOCKS
■■■■■■■■■■

■ Question 1: Define prayer:
   a. In your own words.

b. Through the definition of a dictionary.

c. Through a biblical reference source.

d. What similarities or discrepancies did you notice between the definitions?

■ Question 2: There are different types of prayers and different reasons for prayer. Look up the following verses and describe the type of prayer each one represents.
a. 1 Samuel 1:10-17

b. 2 Chronicles 7:14

c. Job 42:8

d. Daniel 9:1-19

■ Question 3: One of the greatest examples of all prayers is given to us by Jesus himself in Matthew 6:9-13. When His disciples asked Him how to pray, He gave them this model, known as the Lord's Prayer, to follow.
a. Describe what each verse of this prayer means to you.

b. Write your own personal prayer using the Lord's Prayer as a model.

■ Question 4: What does Jesus specifically tell us not to do in prayer?
a. Matthew 6:5

b. Matthew 6:7

c. Give an example of how both are handled incorrectly today.

■ Question 5: What are some "do's" that should be a part of our prayers and in our attitudes of prayer?
a. Psalm 145:18

b. 1 Thessalonians 5:18

c. 1 Timothy 2:8

d. Hebrews 10:22

e. 1 John 5:14

■ Question 6: What are the desires of your heart? Write a prayer incorporating praise, protection, and peace with each desire you identify.

■ Question 7: From the desires of your heart, find promises to pray in God's will. Write them down and make a commitment to pray them every day.

Chapter 7

WHEN GOD SPEAKS, ARE YOU LISTENING?

Practicing Hearing God's Voice, Part 1

I (BOBBYE) INTRODUCED YOU TO MY BASSET HOUND, Buddy, who knows me, and he knows my voice, without a doubt, because I have a certain way of talking to him. Even if he's far away from me, and he hears my voice, he knows it's me and he comes running. My youngest sister raised basset hounds before I did, and she just loves Buddy. She wants Buddy to love her too, so every time she visited me after I first got Buddy, she would call to him and try to get him to come to her. But Buddy is very skittish around people he doesn't know, and at the beginning he wasn't coming to her because he didn't recognize her voice. She was a stranger to him.

Finally one day I told her, "Jill, you know how to talk to dogs. Just talk to Buddy," so she got down on the floor and started talking to him, and each time she visited me she would do that.

Jill and I sound a lot alike even though she has more of a Southern accent than I do, and it didn't take very long for that dog to start to recognize her voice. After that, when he heard her, he just melted.

WHAT WOULD OUR LIVES BE LIKE IF WE COULD DISCERN SO CLEARLY THE VOICE OF GOD IN OUR HEARTS AND OUR MINDS VERSUS A STRANGER'S VOICE?

Now she's no longer a stranger to him because even in his dog mind, he is able to discern her voice. Anytime she calls out to him, "Buddy, come here," he runs to her. There's a familiarity there; he recognizes her voice.

What would our lives be like if we could discern so clearly the voice of God in our hearts and our minds versus a stranger's voice? What if we could immediately recognize that it is God speaking to us, and respond by "running" to Him? Would your life be different if you knew every day that whatever you asked of God you could hear Him tell you the answer or at least talk to you about what to do? Absolutely it would. I believe it can be that way, but it doesn't come without much practice and prayer.

Have you ever wondered if you were hearing God's voice? I could count on both hands the times I really thought I heard Him speaking to me for probably the first thirty years of my life. But most of the time I just wasn't sure. I would hear His voice (in my heart) at times when I was definitely seeking Him the most, but it took many years for me to have an ongoing ability to hear His voice on a daily basis and know it is Him speaking—and I'm still learning.

Hearing God speak to us is an important part of practicing His presence because when we can recognize His voice, we can receive what He's trying to tell us about His blessings, plans, and purpose for our lives. So I am going to lay a foundation for you of what I've learned over the years on how we can know for sure—the best that we can know in our limited bodies and minds—that we are hearing the voice of our heavenly Father.

The difficulty with Christians today is not that they don't hear God's voice but that they cannot discern the Lord's voice over all the other voices they hear. This is why practicing God's presence is so important to hearing and understanding His voice, which is why we purposely placed this section near the end of our book.

If you truly learn to have a heart of worship and then choose to pray in accordance to God's Word (His will), you will have no difficulty in learning how to practice His presence in hearing His voice—but it's a process.

As we learn to practice God's presence through worship and prayer, we learn to shut out the distractions of the world. It doesn't take long for us to yearn to be with the Lord in that intimate place of worship where only He reigns and nothing or no one else matters. Then by practicing His presence through prayer, we learn to communicate with the Lord as He leads us to find His will for our lives, not just tell Him our selfish desires. Once we are in that place, prayer becomes a two-way form of communication—not only do we speak to God, but He speaks back to us and we know His voice.

We can be sure that hearing God's voice is His will for us because He has been speaking since the beginning of time as we know it. As you read the Bible, you will see that God really spoke to His people. The Scriptures, starting with Genesis in the Old Testament, are filled with stories, testimonies, and experiences to help us understand this better. Basically, God begins explaining in Genesis 2 how He developed a relationship with man before sin—remember how God spoke with Adam in the Garden, and then in Genesis 3, how the relationship changed after sin entered?

> PRAYER BECOMES A TWO-WAY FORM OF COMMUNICATION—NOT ONLY DO WE SPEAK TO GOD, BUT HE SPEAKS BACK TO US AND WE KNOW HIS VOICE.

The relationship changed, but God's desires and intents never changed. He went to great lengths and showed much mercy as He continued to reach out to man as evidenced by the stories in the Bible. It has been said that the acronym for the word, B-i-b-l-e is "Basic Instruction Before Leaving Earth." If we believe that the Bible is God's instruction book for us, then we need to read it to understand how God related to His people in the past to appreciate His relationship with us today.

GOD NOT ONLY SPOKE TO HIS PEOPLE IN BIBLE DAYS, BUT HE HAS NEVER STOPPED SPEAKING.

God not only spoke to His people in Bible days, but He has never stopped speaking because He desires to dwell with us, to walk with us, to talk with us—to have a relationship with us. He is speaking to us, His people, today as well because having a relationship takes communication.

Look at how much we have to say as human beings. We spend most of our time communicating through our voices. If God created us and made us in His image—the image of the Father, Son, and Holy Spirit (Genesis 1:26 AMP)—then simple logic should tell us that we serve a God who not only created our voices, but did so because He understands this form of communication himself.

The real issue of hearing God's voice is not about Him not talking to us. It involves whether or not we know how to hear what He is saying.

TWO-WAY COMMUNICATION

It seems clear that right from the start God had a way of speaking to someone so that they clearly understood Him. We already saw how God spoke to Adam in the Garden of Eden, and God continued to speak to His people even after the fall. He spoke to Cain and asked what happened to his brother Abel. Cain and God had a conversation about Abel's whereabouts, and God sentenced Cain to a life of being a fugitive (Genesis 4:9-12).

God spoke to Noah and told him that He was going to flood the earth because it was full of evil and corruption, and God instructed Noah to build an ark, giving him the dimensions and details in Genesis 6:14-21. Why did God choose to speak to Noah as opposed to someone else? Noah was a just man who found grace in the eyes of the Lord. (See Genesis 6:8-9.) That means "he was in all things a consistent character, never departing from the truth in principle or practice. He walked with God—he was not only righteous [morally right or good] in his conduct, but he...had continual communion with God."[1]

Through the grace of Christ we are blessed with the presence of God (when we become born again) and can hear His voice in our hearts as clearly as Noah did. *Grace* is the "unmerited divine assistance"[2] God gives to us. It means "favour, acceptance;"[3] the "good will, loving-kindness...by which God...keeps, strengthens, [and] increases [His children] in Christian faith, knowledge, affection, and kindles them to the exercise of the Christian virtues."[4] Only through grace can we enter into God's holy presence and hear Him speaking to us.

ONLY THROUGH GRACE CAN WE ENTER INTO GOD'S HOLY PRESENCE AND HEAR HIM SPEAKING TO US.

Later on, God chose a nation of people to call His own. This nation became God's chosen race, the Israelites, and through His appointed leaders, prophets, and priests, God spoke. The father of this nation was Abraham, who like Noah often heard God speak to him. For instance, God told Abraham to leave his country, that He was going to make a great nation out of Abraham, and that He would bless Abraham and bless those who blessed him (Genesis 12:1-4).

From Abraham came Isaac and from Isaac came Jacob. Abraham, Isaac, and Jacob (whose name was later changed to Israel) are known as the Patriarchs, or founding fathers of the nation of Israel. In Genesis 26:1-5, God spoke to Isaac during a famine and told him not to go to Egypt but to dwell in the land He would show him. In Genesis 31:11, God spoke to Jacob in a dream. Down through the generations God spoke to others like Moses who was called by God when He appeared to him in the burning bush. (See Exodus 3:2.)

God clearly manifested himself to these and certain other people in the Old Testament. They heard His voice and knew Him personally. Let's look at some other ways God spoke to His people.

There came a time, while Moses was leading the children of Israel to the Promised Land, that the people didn't want to hear God's voice. God had told Moses that He was going to speak directly to His people, but they must prepare themselves first. (See Exodus 19.) When they were ready, God came down upon Mount Sinai in a thick cloud of smoke and fire. Then He personally gave His people the Ten Commandments by speaking the commandments to them out loud (Exodus 20:1-17).

After God finished speaking, the people were terribly afraid of all that they had seen and heard. Maybe they were not prepared for such a display of God's awesome power and might, but their response was clear. They did not want to hear the Lord's voice like that anymore.

Now all the people witnessed the thunderings, the lightning flashes, the sound of the trumpet, and the mountain smoking; and when the people saw it, they trembled and stood afar off. Then they said to Moses, "You speak with us, and we will hear; but let not God speak with us, lest we die." And Moses said to the people, "Do not fear; for God has come to test you, and that His fear may be before you, so that you may not sin."

—Exodus 20:18-20

The Israelites wanted a mediator to speak on their behalf, so God continued to talk to them through Moses. After they entered the Promised Land and settled into their territories, God sent His Angel to speak to certain judges that He raised up to lead the people. Various accounts in Scripture tell us that the Angel of the Lord spoke to a number of people like that. These kinds of specific references to the Angel of the Lord are called a *theophany*, which is a "manifestation of God that is tangible to the human senses."[5]

For instance, in Judges 6:11-23, the Angel of the Lord appeared to Gideon and called him a mighty man of valor. In Judges 13:3, we also see that the Angel of the Lord appeared to a barren woman, the wife of Manoah, telling her that she would have a son, that he was to be named Samson, and that he would later become a great deliverer of Israel.

The only other people who were in close fellowship with the Lord during this time were His priests and prophets. Samuel, who was called as a youth, was one such prophet, and God had a specific purpose for his life.

Samuel anointed Israel's first king whose name was Saul, but Saul did not hear God's voice directly like Samuel did. We learn from 1 Samuel 28:6 that God did not speak to Saul ... *by dreams or by Urim or by the prophets.* Years later, a youth named David was tending his father's sheep when Samuel the prophet was directed by the Lord to anoint him king, replacing Saul. Scripture tells us that David was known as a man after God's own heart (1 Samuel 13:14).

Many of the psalms were written by David, expressing his heart of worship and love for the Lord, but even though David had God's heart, David did not seem to hear God's voice audibly like Samuel (the prophet) but more like Saul (the king). Although David received the Lord's messages through different forms of communication, the power of the Lord's Spirit was just as personal and intimate to David.

You have to remember, though, that at this point in time Jesus had not come to fulfill all of the requirements that were needed for

God to speak freely with His people. God's Spirit would come upon certain people from time to time but did not dwell in their hearts because the atonement for sin had yet to be accomplished through Jesus. So acts of ritualistic obedience had to be adhered to before God would speak to His people, just as the children of Israel had to prepare before God spoke the Ten Commandments to them.

HAVING A PERSONAL RELATIONSHIP WITH THE LORD IS AVAILABLE TO ALL, NOT JUST TO THE PROPHETS AND PRIESTS.

The tabernacle was God's dwelling place at that time, and the daily sacrifices were required for forgiveness of sin, along with numerous daily rituals performed there by the Levites and priests. Everything God established during this period of time was to make the way for Jesus' coming.

The second half of the Old Testament consists of the writings of several of God's prophets who foretold significant events, including the coming of the Messiah, the future of the Israelites, and the final end-time events (still yet to be fulfilled). The majority of these prophecies were fulfilled when Jesus came to earth and restored our relationship with God so that we could worship Him and fellowship with Him freely.

Having a personal relationship with the Lord is available to all, not just to the prophets and priests. There is no need for a sacrificial system anymore for Jesus became the ultimate sacrifice. There is no more need for a hierarchy of priests because Jesus, the perfect Man, bridged the gap permanently for us to worship individually. John 1:14 KJV says that *the Word* [Jesus] *was made flesh, and dwelt* [or tabernacled] *among us....* It is because of Jesus that we find a place of intimacy and two-way fellowship with God that cannot be found anywhere else.

TUNED IN TO GOD

When we are in a place of worship, we also put ourselves in a place of prayer. Proof of that can be seen in the life of the psalmist David. While he was out in the wilderness by himself, tending his father's flocks of sheep, he would often worship God by singing songs to Him. David would also pray to hear God's voice and ask Him for guidance and deliverance.

WE ACTUALLY CAN *HEAR* GOD'S LOVINGKINDNESS AND MERCY.

> *Cause me to hear Your lovingkind-*
> *ness in the morning,*
> *For in You do I trust;*
> *Cause me to know the way in which I should walk,*
> *For I lift up my soul to You.*
>
> —Psalm 143:8

We know from the Word that God heard and answered David's prayer. But I especially like how David described in this verse what we can hear when we talk to God, saying that we actually can *hear* God's lovingkindness and mercy. I'm not always sure we relate *hearing* mercy or *hearing* love to God. We may sense it or feel it, but David is saying that to hear it we need to start our day in that place of knowing.

Does that sound familiar? It goes back to what we've already seen in this book—before we ever leave our house in the morning we should spend time with the Lord. Then we've attuned ourselves to hearing and discerning His voice, and we've got our senses back in line with Him because we need to know which way to walk throughout the day.

Jesus described discerning God's voice to His disciples in a way that was familiar to the people of that day. He talked about a shepherd and how he guides his sheep.

"To him the doorkeeper opens, and the sheep hear his voice; and he calls his own sheep by name and leads them out. And when he brings out his own sheep, he goes before them; and the sheep follow him, for they know his voice. Yet they will by no means follow a stranger, but will flee from him, for they do not know the voice of strangers.... My sheep hear My voice, and I know them, and they follow Me."

—John 10:3-5, 27

This is a familiar passage to many from the gospel of John, but it points out that God is speaking and He wants us to know and recognize His voice. Our God does not desire to be separated from us; it's all about relationship with Him. Jesus came for us and has given us the privilege today to know our heavenly Father and to hear His voice as clearly as anyone ever did in the past, just as the sheep know the voice of their shepherd. So the question is not, "Is God talking to us?" but "Are we listening and recognizing His voice?"

GOD DOES NOT DESIRE TO BE SEPARATED FROM US; IT'S ALL ABOUT RELATIONSHIP WITH HIM.

When we hear God's voice in our heart, we can have many different thoughts come into our mind as we hear Him speaking to us. Really we use the word *hear* loosely in this context because while most of the Bible translations for verses like John 10:27 use the word *hear*, several translations (the *New International Version*, for example) use the word *listen*. Is there a difference between hearing and listening? I believe there is.

If you attended one of the conferences that Tonilee and I hold, and I was speaking, you would be hearing my voice, but I'm not sure if you would be really listening to me. You probably would be looking at me, so I would assume that you were listening to me and that I had your undivided attention. Yet, you could be sitting there looking at me and hearing me but have ten thoughts going through your mind at the same time.

Now some of us take pride in that. We consider we're working as we're sitting there in a Bible study. For instance, you may think, *It's great that I've been able to get my whole day planned out. Now I can tune in the last two minutes of Bobbye's message.* Can you relate to that? Do you see how easy it is to tune in and out when someone is speaking to you? That's what people often do, and it is one of the pitfalls of being in this body of flesh and trying to hear the voice of God. It's a kind of distraction that we need to overcome.

WE HAVE A RESPONSIBILITY TO PRACTICE AND DISCERN GOD'S VOICE— HEARING IS THE EASY PART; LISTENING TAKES PRACTICE.

Overcoming distractions is just one of the issues we deal with in practicing hearing God's voice because we are not perfect. So often we struggle with it because we are not constantly walking in the Spirit. (See Romans 8:4-5.) That's why we have a responsibility to practice and discern God's voice—hearing is the easy part; listening takes practice.

Many times when the Bible talks about God listening to us, it says He inclines His ear to hear us. (See Psalm 40:1.) To *incline* is to bend forward and listen intently to the person who is speaking.[6] In the same way, when we are *listening* to God speak to us, it means that we are very aware that He is speaking to us. *Listening* means that we are putting ourselves in that place of inclining our ear to give the Lord our undivided attention to hear His voice.

I like the part of John 10:5 when Jesus says that the sheep who hear a stranger's voice run away. Wouldn't that be great if we could so clearly discern the stranger's voice—the Enemy, Satan—that we knew when he was clearly talking to us and say, "That's not the voice of my God; I'm not listening to that!" because we knew who to listen to and to run to so quickly?

The truth is that we have so many other voices and distractions coming at us that sometimes we may think, *I'm not sure if that was really God. Would He really be telling me that?*

When we hear God speaking to us, we may even start thinking we're crazy. I know there are some people who would be glad to tell us we're crazy! Tonilee and I have received lots of "encouragement" in that way. The moment you say that God told you something, especially if what He told you to do is really unusual, those kinds of people look at you like you've lost your mind.

I remember when Tonilee and I had become prayer partners and in a short period of time of praying together, we knew God was calling us to work together as a ministry team. One of the first things He led us to do was to write a 23-week Bible study on the Book of 1 Corinthians for the church study. We were new at this, but we kept moving along and made sure we stayed in a place of prayer continually. We wanted to be sure we were really hearing God's voice.

When we wrote the study on 1 Corinthians, many people we knew told us we were crazy. Now we knew God had put it on our hearts to write it, and we had confirmation in His Word, but there were times when we had to get new confirmations from God that we had heard His voice about it because when people keep telling you that you're crazy to do something like that, it's very easy to start believing them at some point.

When you walk with God and you hear His voice, you will sometimes do things clearly in faith because God is telling you to do them. No one else may necessarily be agreeing, but that's why you must make every effort to stay in that place of worship and prayer, practicing God's presence, and knowing how to hear His voice. If you're too concerned with what others think, you may totally miss what God is trying to do with you.

STEPS TO HEARING GOD

God has a purpose for your life that He wants to talk to you about, but you can't understand heavenly things until your eyes are opened spiritually. Once your eyes are open, the Lord can direct you, guide you, and speak to you through His Holy Spirit.

Jesus tells us that *"He who belongs to God hears what God says. The reason you do not hear is that you do not belong to God"* (John 8:47 NIV). He had said that to very religious men who studied the laws and commandments of God. They dedicated their lives to knowing God's ways, but somehow they did not *know* Him—they had no relationship with Him. So the first step in hearing God's voice is to know Him personally—not know about Him or attempt to live for Him, but to have a relationship with Him. This has been the essence of what we've been covering in this book.

It goes back to the fact that Jesus came to earth for us to know Him personally. By accepting Jesus as our Savior (saving us from our sins) and Lord (willing to follow His commandments as Master over our daily lives), we receive His Holy Spirit. It is *only* through the Spirit of God that we can be sensitive to God's voice.

JESUS CAME TO EARTH FOR US TO KNOW HIM PERSONALLY.

The only way that we can hear God's voice is to have His Holy Spirit inside of us. If we truly believe and know and receive the power of His Holy Spirit, then we have the ability to hear God in any way He chooses to speak to us—through people, circumstances, impressions we feel on the inside of us, and our thoughts, to name a few. The problem is that we are limited because we are flesh and blood, and we are weak in our own selves—we are doubtful and fearful and insecure. So we need to have a way of knowing and testing and going back to a foundation of how God is talking to us to be sure it's really Him.

How does God speak? How do we know that it is the Lord?

Even the Old Testament prophet Samuel had a difficult time learning to discern God's voice while working in His temple. (See 1 Samuel 3:3-8.) Today God speaks to us through His Word, the Bible, as the Holy Spirit opens our minds to comprehend the Scriptures (Luke 24:45). That is the next step in hearing God's voice. We have found that you can read the words of the Bible and gain knowledge of what the Bible says, or you can read the Bible and hear the voice of God speaking to your heart.

THE LISTENING PROCESS BEGINS BY READING AND MEDITATING ON GOD'S WORD.

Let me (Tonilee) assure you that you can come to the Word and open it and seek answers, not leaving the Word until you know that the very hand of God has touched you. You can knock so loudly and so persistently that you know God has opened the door of your heart to come in and dine with you (Revelation 3:20). When you reach that place of intimacy with the Lord, you can get up from the floor or from sitting on the bed or from the desk or wherever you've been seeking God and have His peace reigning in your heart in such a way that regardless of any circumstance you go through, you just know that He can carry you through it on eagle's wings.

We talked about listening earlier, but the listening process begins by reading and meditating on God's Word. The more we read, the more we keep His Word in our heart. His words that are placed within our heart and mind are the key to hearing His voice. You can be sure that His voice will not contradict His Word, and His Word is applicable for everything in our lives.

My (Bobbye) oldest sister, Diane, has an adorable granddaughter, and she bought her a children's Bible which they had been reading together at night. One time when they were out in my sister's car, it began acting up in some way and they had a problem with it. When they got home, my sister took the owner's manual out of the glove compartment and she started looking up how to fix her car. Her granddaughter asked what she was doing and she said, "I'm looking up how to fix my car." Suddenly her granddaughter said, "I'll be right back," and ran in the house.

Soon she came back with her little children's Bible and holding it up, she said to my sister, "Whatever you need to fix your car is in this Book. This Book will tell you how to fix your car." Diane smiled and lovingly brushed her off.

The next morning my sister got up and was eating breakfast. She was on a diet and her granddaughter came into the kitchen with that children's Bible and said, "Grandma, this Book will tell you how to diet. You want to lose weight, just read this Book."

This story shows the faith of a little child, the kind of faith Jesus said we should have (Matthew 18:3), but the point is, this little girl is right—everything you need is in the Bible. It's the key to hearing and knowing God's voice.

MORE THAN JUST STORIES

All Scripture is given by inspiration of God, and is profitable for doctrine, for reproof, for correction, for instruction in righteousness, that the man of God may be complete, thoroughly equipped for every good work.

—2 Timothy 3:16-17

In 2 Timothy 3 the apostle Paul was writing a letter to Timothy, whom Paul considered to be his own *son in the faith* (1 Timothy 1:2). Paul wanted the people to understand that the Holy Scriptures were written by man, but inspired by God. God breathed the Word; man wrote it down. If this Word, the Bible, has always existed, that means God already knew about everything that happened that is written in this Word *before* it ever happened. Before man ever wrote it down, the Bible has always been, and it's full of history and stories.

We could take the Bible at face value and think of it as just a story,

THE WORD IS MORE THAN JUST STORIES THAT WERE WRITTEN DOWN.

as words written on a page that tell us about God's people, about God, and about Jesus. If we look at it from that perspective, we will learn how to live. We will gain a lot of knowledge if we just read it for what it is. Even if we believe it is only a good story, we will know so much more about how to live life. But the Word is more than just stories that were written down that man tries to date back to a specific period of time and place.

> *In the beginning was the Word, and the Word was with God, and the Word was God. He was in the beginning with God. All things were made through Him, and without Him nothing was made that was made.*
> —John 1:1-3

In this passage the words *He* and *Him* are symbolic of the Word of God, and verse 1 tells us that this Word existed before the foundation of the world. How can that be? How is that possible? The Word is more than pages of a book.

> *The Word became flesh and dwelt among us.*
> —John 1:14

This verse "denotes the essential Word of God, Jesus Christ... the cause of all the world's life both physical and ethical."[7] In other words, Jesus is the Word, and this Word is more alive than we are. He is power, life, and Spirit.

When we have the Holy Spirit living on the inside of us and we read and study and mediate on the Word, the Holy Spirit has something to work with in us, particularly in our thoughts. Something in your heart can draw you to read a verse or passage or chapter in the Bible that you've read every day for the last ten days, and God's Spirit can speak to you through it somehow and bless you and teach you something different from it each time you read it.

I (Bobbye) love the Old Testament, but I spent so much of my life feeling just the opposite about it. I just wanted to hear about Jesus, not anything in the Old Testament. I didn't realize back then that the whole Bible is filled with Scriptures about Jesus. I thought that the Old Testament wasn't relevant for today. But when God starts speaking to you about something like a tabernacle that in the natural has nothing to do with anything in your life, it can become relevant to you (spiritually) because the Holy Spirit can take whatever we've read in the Word and put it in us in a way that it begins to stir us.

THE HOLY SPIRIT CAN TAKE WHATEVER WE'VE READ IN THE WORD AND PUT IT IN US IN A WAY THAT IT BEGINS TO STIR US.

Let's say that you spend some time with God each morning and you open the Word and read your daily devotional. Then you pray and you go on about your day. If you've read anything in the Word, God can bring it back to you at some point because reading the Bible is not just reading a book, comprehending it, and thinking about a message. This Word is life and power that comes off the pages. This Word is joy and peace and love and hope and everything else we need.

You have to be in the Word regularly to hear and know God's voice. I'm not talking about just obligatory reading here. I'm talking about loving the Word and eating it up. The prophet Jeremiah refers to it like this:

> *Your words were found, and I ate them,*
> *And Your word was to me the joy and rejoicing of my heart.*
> —Jeremiah 15:16

We should see the Word as daily bread that we eat. As we take it in, it becomes a part of us and affects us—strengthening, sustaining, giving life—just as the natural foods that we eat affect us. It can do that in us just by reading it.

WE SHOULD SEE THE WORD AS DAILY BREAD THAT WE EAT.

A FIRM FOUNDATION

I (Bobbye) spent a lot of my life having absolutely no interest in reading the Word except when I needed to, even though I was raised in church and loved the Lord. I grew up in Sunday school so I knew all the Bible stories and I memorized verses, but I can't say I was really drawn to reading the Bible every day. There would be weeks when I would never open my Bible except on Sunday mornings. It took going through a series of trials in my life, when circumstances beyond my control began to happen to me, for me to get to the point where I felt I had nothing to lose by reading the Word.

I decided to start reading it every day. I even decided to go on a fast (and at that time I wasn't big on fasting), but I was in a desperate situation. I was leaving my career. Everything in my life that I had planned was literally slipping through my fingers, and I was desperate. This God I had known my whole life, Who blessed me and answered my prayers so many times before, seemed to just stop doing any of that, and I was not happy. Something was wrong, so I finally decided to try reading the Bible.

I declared a forty-day fast from television and the news and all that I enjoyed so much, and I started reading in Genesis and was determined to read through the whole Bible for the first time in my life. I thought it would be a struggle just to read through the Old Testament, but as I started, I couldn't believe what happened. I knew the stories from Sunday school, but all of a sudden, as I began to read in Genesis, they had a whole new meaning of what God was doing. What it did for me was teach me so much about who God is.

I thought I knew God, knew His Son, knew His ways because I had been born again since I was a child, but as I read through the Old Testament, I realized that I didn't have a clue. Every morning I'd get up and I'd read and I'd write down on a notepad certain verses and certain prayers while I was reading. I kept a daily record so I could look back and see the progress I was making.

I remember one day it seemed as though the words jumped off the page at me and ministered to me about something I was dealing with in my life at the time. The story was about the man named Naboth who had a vineyard, and King Ahab and Queen Jezebel wanted his vineyard. (See 1 Kings 21.) As I was reading, the story just hit me because it applied to me and something I was dealing with at the time. I was so surprised to find the answer I was looking for in that story, but a whole learning process began in my life of seeing God and hearing Him through His Word like never before.

As I continued my daily Bible reading, I began to have thoughts related to what I had read come in my mind at the strangest times. I would be doing something like cooking or laundry and all of a sudden I would have one of these thoughts pop in my mind, and I'd wonder where that thought came from. Sometimes I'd wake up in the middle of the night having a dream or having these kinds of thoughts, and I would get up and say, "Is that You, Lord? Prove it to me; show me in Your Word if that thought is from You," because I had been taught that you should ... *test the spirits, whether they are of God* (1 John 4:1). I didn't want any thoughts from deceiving spirits coming into my mind so I'd tell the Lord, "I've got to know, and Your Word is the only way I can know."

I was so young in the Lord, but yet that's exactly where I needed to be, and soon after that, I found the verses in 1 John 2:20, 27 that say the Holy Spirit will teach us all things we need to know. I

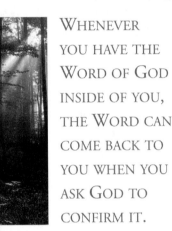

WHENEVER YOU HAVE THE WORD OF GOD INSIDE OF YOU, THE WORD CAN COME BACK TO YOU WHEN YOU ASK GOD TO CONFIRM IT.

got so excited I said, "Lord, You've got to teach me. I've got to know it all." I began to write down any of these kinds of thoughts and every time—maybe it was a day later, maybe it was a week later, or a month or more later—but whatever I wrote down and asked God to confirm through His Word, He would do it. He didn't always do it the way I thought, and it wasn't always in my timing, but He always brought back to me the confirmation through His Word and the Holy Spirit.

See, the Holy Spirit is always bringing things to our minds. We have thoughts all the time that are Him speaking to us; we're just not recognizing the voice of God. How much are we missing that He's saying to us but we don't give Him credit for because we get so caught up in our daily lives and so tripped up with distractions? That happened to me, but by God's grace I moved past it only because I kept going back to the Word.

Whenever you have the Word of God inside of you, the Word can come back to you when you ask God to confirm it. So the way to test that it is God speaking to you is through the old standby—the Word. That's why the Word is so very important. We have seen that the Word is one of the spiritual weapons God has given us to speak in prayer. Another purpose of the Word is to be the foundation that we can go back to for verification when anything comes at us to make us doubt that we've heard from God.

Here's another point to remember. There may be times in your life when you are absolutely certain that God has told you something and you have verses to prove it, but it seems as though what He's told you doesn't happen. Does that mean God wasn't talking to you? Does that mean that you were deceived? No, you need to keep going back to the foundation of the Word because if the Enemy can plant any doubt in you, that's probably one of the biggest and most powerful ways he'll do it.

We may go down a path of believing that God has so clearly shown us something, but it doesn't happen when we think it should or it changes, and we feel like the rug has been pulled out from under us. So we decide that we aren't going to listen to God anymore. Who's to say that it wasn't God the whole time? If you have verses to confirm it and you were in prayer and you fasted and you had confirmation and you went down that path, most likely it was God speaking to you.

Now if you were talking to psychics, looking at Ouija boards, or doing any other kind of ungodly action, that definitely wasn't God. When you commit yourself to seeking God's will and following all the ways His Word teaches us, you are still in line with Him. But remember that He is God and He can do whatever He pleases—He can take His time to make something happen or He can even change our course—but He always works everything together for our good (Romans 8:28).

REMEMBER, GOD CAN DO WHATEVER HE PLEASES—BUT HE ALWAYS WORKS EVERYTHING TOGETHER FOR OUR GOOD.

What are you going to do if you find yourself in that place?

Sometimes we get to the point in life when we are on the threshold of receiving so much more that God has for us, but because our foolproof method didn't work and it all didn't go according to our plan, we get into doubt and unbelief and may even think that we really didn't hear from the Lord. If you find yourself in that kind of situation, don't forget that sometimes we go through trials and we get tested. Yet it's in some of those places of trials, those times of testing, that we get to know God better and learn more about His character than when we're just cruising along in life—and it's in those places that our foundation really needs to be in the Word because that's where we'll find everything we need for victorious living.

BUILDING BLOCKS
■■■■■■■■■

■ Question 1: Take a moment and write down your personal views on how you hear God's voice.

   a. How does the Lord speak to you personally?

   b. How do you know it is the Lord's voice?

   c. What do you want to learn from this lesson?

■ Question 2: God has been speaking since the beginning of time as we know it. How did the event described in Genesis 3:8-19 change the communication between God and man?

■ Question 3: The next person in Scripture that God spoke to was Noah.

   a. Why did God choose to speak to Noah as opposed to someone else? (See Genesis 6:8-9.)

   b. How does that same reason apply to our lives today in hearing God's voice?

■ Question 4: From Exodus 19:16-24, answer the following questions.

   a. What did the Lord require of the people before they could come near?

   b. How would these requirements apply to us today as Christians?

■ Question 5: How do you think you would have reacted to the Lord's presence on Mount Sinai? How do you sense His presence in your life today?

Chapter 8

WHEN GOD SPEAKS, ARE YOU LISTENING?

Practicing Hearing God's Voice, Part 2

H EARING GOD'S VOICE IS A TOPIC THAT GREATLY warms my (Tonilee) heart because, as Bobbye said in the last chapter, the Lord wants to speak to each of us individually. He wants us to know His voice. He wants us to know His plans for us. Yet even though as Christians we know that God can speak to us, we can still wonder at times if it's really Him.

A few years ago a Christian woman I knew very well had that same concern. She called me to ask if I would meet with her privately and sounded very serious, but she didn't tell me what it was about so I wasn't sure what she wanted. I had heard her talk about the Lord and share the Gospel with others many times, so I thought that maybe she needed something clarified that I had taught or maybe I said something in the wrong way and I needed to apologize.

When we finally met, the first thing she said to me was, "I have some questions for you," and then she explained to me that for a while her husband had been pulling away from her and she sensed that he had been committing adultery. She noticed that he wouldn't communicate as well with her like he used to, he seemed aloof, and he wasn't really committed to their relationship anymore. His plans seemed to be changing for their lives, and it was making her feel very unsettled.

She didn't want to tell anybody because he was active in their church, so she told me that all she could do was seek the Lord. "Tonilee, I started reading the Bible and praying. I asked God what was happening, and I asked Him to show me what was in my husband's heart and what path I was heading down in this relationship." Then she said, "I am telling you that there were verses in the Bible that popped out at me so greatly that I knew I was supposed to pick up a piece of paper my husband had shredded in the trash can. When I taped that paper together, it turned out to be a love letter to his girlfriend."

What bothered my friend the most was that every time she turned to the Word, she heard God tell her what to do next, and slowly He started opening her eyes to what was going on in her marriage. When she met with me, her husband was at the point where he wouldn't even communicate with her anymore, and she didn't know what to do, yet she said to me, "That's not my question. My question is, am I crazy? Can the Word of God talk to me that clearly? Can I really come to the Word and know step by step the plans that God has for me and be led by Him in this way? I keep wondering if there's something wrong with me."

Actually that's exactly how it is to walk with the Lord. You can come to the Word of God, and it can lead you and answer every question you have. When I told her this, she said, "So this is what you mean when you talk about hearing God's voice and coming to His Word."

You have to understand that at this time she had known the Lord for more than twenty years, so her statement shocked me and I asked her, "Haven't you ever experienced this in your Christian life? All those times when you have said 'The Lord told me' and 'I was in the Word' you never really sensed His presence and that He was talking to you personally?" To my amazement she said no.

I couldn't believe that it had taken a terrible problem like adultery for her to really seek the Lord and to find out that He could speak to her in the Word, and it made me realize that even active, serving Christians don't always know how to hear from God. It took a painful situation for her to finally learn how to hear God's voice, but sometimes our heart has to be in that humble, broken, and contrite place in order for God to get our undivided attention.

Over the years I (Tonilee) have gone through trials and terrible situations, but I am so thankful that I know what it is to be in the presence of God and to hear His voice. It has made all the difference. I know now why the Bible says to taste and see that the Lord is good because when you're in that place of such intimacy and relationship with Him, you almost feel as if you can taste His presence. It is such a privilege and honor and blessing, not to mention humbling, to be there on a daily basis, no matter what is going on in your circumstances.

GOD HONORS AND BLESSES THOSE WHO BELIEVE WITHOUT SEEING. YET A LIFE OF FAITH DOES NOT MEAN THAT WE WALK AROUND SPIRITUALLY BLIND, DEAF, AND DUMB.

Our Christian life is a walk of faith. We may never see anything spiritual or be able to cling to God with our earthly arms. We will never read a letter written personally to us from God or answer the phone with the Lord on the other end giving us instructions on what He wants next. Why? Because God honors and blesses those who believe without seeing. Yet a life of faith does not mean that we walk around spiritually blind, deaf, and dumb. As our faith is tested and tried, we come to a place of power and inner confidence that what we believe is so real and true that we can abandon all to follow the Lord.

GOD WILL SOMETIMES USE OUR PROBLEMS TO TEST US.

God will sometimes use our problems to test us (Psalm 17:3). Although He is not the source of our troubles, He wants to see where our heart is and if we will stay with Him regardless of the situation. Here is an example from the Word of a man who practiced God's presence until he faced a difficult trial.

Asa was a good king of Judah, and the Bible says that the nation was at rest and had no wars for many years because Asa sought God. (See 2 Chronicles 14:6-7; 15:15.) He was faithful to God even to the point of taking down and destroying the pagan idols, altars, and shrines that the Israelites were worshiping. Then suddenly things changed—Asa made a treaty with Syria instead of relying on God.

> *At that time Hanani the seer came to Asa king of Judah, and said to him: "Because you have relied on the king of Syria, and have not relied on the LORD your God, therefore the army of the king of Syria has escaped from your hand. Were the Ethiopians and the Lubim not a huge army with very many chariots and horsemen? Yet, because you relied on the LORD, He delivered them into your hand. For the eyes of the LORD run to and fro throughout the whole earth, to show Himself strong on behalf of those whose heart is loyal to Him. In this you have done foolishly; therefore from now on you shall have wars."*
>
> —2 Chronicles 16:7-9

Asa had much peace and rest in his life, but then the king of Israel came against him. God used that situation to test Asa to see if he was still with Him and still willing to thank Him for all the blessings he had been enjoying, but Asa didn't do that. He turned from trusting God at that point and instead trusted in Syria. He got angry with

Hanani who brought him the message in this passage, and he ended up losing that war and dying a bitter man, seeking the counsel of men instead of the counsel of God.

The Christian life can seem hard at times because in some seasons of life every step you take feels like, "Lord, another trial? Another circumstance to overcome?" Yet trials get our attention and turn us to God, and we can be blessed through them. When we get to the point that we can look beyond the circumstances and say, "Lord, no matter what happens, I am staying with You," God can greatly bless us because we have chosen to keep our faith and to be obedient to Him, and He knows that our character is strong enough to receive all the good things He has for us.

I (Tonilee) had two miscarriages in a row before I gave birth to my first son. That was a very hard trial to go through, but during that time I had a choice to make: *Do I still want God? Is He still going to be first in my life? Am I still going to be wholly devoted to Him?* My answer was yes, and eventually my son was born.

Now God didn't cause those miscarriages. The devil is the one who steals, kills, and destroys (John 10:10). But looking back over that season of my life, I realized that when we're in a difficult situation, it all comes down to this: God can change every circumstance in your life and He can remove all the adversaries, and He will. But He often uses adverse circumstances to test your heart and to change you. He will enable you to live in those circumstances with His help, as He deals with them.

> GOD OFTEN USES ADVERSE CIRCUMSTANCES TO TEST YOUR HEART AND TO CHANGE YOU.

Are you facing some adversity in your life? You may need to ask yourself if you are still seeking the Lord or if you have turned away from Him. Or perhaps you know that you have some "high places" in your life that you just don't want to take down—it's Jesus and that other thing too. But when you can say, "Jesus, I do want You and all that You have for me, so please help me to remove anything that is keeping me from putting You first," it's in that place of honesty that He can come in and work with you and bless you.

GOD IS SO WILLING TO REWARD A HEART THAT COMES TO HIM, HEARS HIM, AND SEEKS HIM.

As you learn how to hear God's voice, you will come to know Him better and to know His purpose for you—and you will understand that He cares more about your relationship with Him than anything else. It all goes back to the condition of our heart. God is so willing to reward a heart that comes to Him, a heart that hears Him, a heart that seeks Him. He loves you so much that He just wants to bless you, but He can't bless you until He knows your heart is right toward Him.

STAY ENCOURAGED

David went through a difficult trial one time when all of his people had turned against him. While he and his men were away fighting in a battle, another enemy had come into his hometown, destroyed it, and captured all their wives and children. When David and his men returned and found that terrible sight, they cried and mourned and were greatly distressed. Then the men blamed David and wanted to stone him to death. What did David do? He encouraged himself in the Lord, and eventually God gave them the victory. They pursued the enemy and recovered all that had been stolen from them (1 Samuel 30).

Walking with the Lord can be difficult and challenging at times, especially in the beginning, so I want to share seven truths that will encourage you when you're trying to seek God and hear His voice and figure out what He is really saying to you.

1. God wants you. That is His desire for you. He absolutely wants you—He wants your attention, He wants your time, He wants your love, He wants your devotion. You will not be disappointed if you give it to Him.

2. God will discipline you or convict you. That is the purpose of the Holy Spirit, to lead us on the right path. We wouldn't go down the right path if we didn't have the Holy Spirit to guide us there. I see that so clearly in my children. If they didn't have my husband and me to direct them in the right way, it would be like herding kittens all the time—they'd just be running in every different direction.

3. God's timing is not yours. God can give you a verse, but it could be three days later (or longer) before you can figure out what He was talking about. There are times when you will know God is speaking to you through a certain verse, but you might hear that verse for weeks or months or even years before you start to understand what God could be telling you because it will be in His timing.

GOD WANTS YOUR ATTENTION, HE WANTS YOUR TIME, HE WANTS YOUR LOVE, HE WANTS YOUR DEVOTION.

For instance, Isaiah tells of the invasion of Judah by the kings of Israel and Syria. They attacked Judah separately (2 Chronicles 28:5-6), then joined each other (2 Kings 16:5), with the objective of displacing Ahaz with another king (Isaiah 7:6). King Ahaz of Judah was afraid. So God sent the prophet Isaiah to tell Ahaz to ask God for a sign because He wanted to show Ahaz the big picture. But Ahaz said, *"I will not ask, nor will I test the LORD"* (v. 12).

Ahaz sounded so righteous and pious by refusing to ask God for a sign, when in fact, he had gone around God and sought help from Assyria's king. When he wouldn't ask God for a sign as Isaiah had instructed him, Isaiah said that God was going to give him a sign anyway. *The Quest Study Bible* explains it thus: "It was a last-ditch offer from God to give Ahaz a way out, saving the nation from needless tragedy—as though the Lord were saying, 'What will it take to prove this to you?' The offer of a sign revealed God's grace and ongoing concern for Judah's destiny."

In verse 14, Isaiah prophesied that a son would be born through a virgin. *The Quest* explains Isaiah 7:14-16, "Like many prophecies, this passage seems to have a double meaning. First, a child, perhaps another son of Isaiah, would be born to a virgin (which could simply refer to a young woman) during the time of Ahaz. By the time he was grown, Judah's two enemies (Israel and Aram) would be destroyed. The second meaning was later applied to the birth of Christ (Matthew 1:23). The name *Immanuel, God with us,* became a title for the Messiah."

GOD'S TIMING IS COMPLETELY DIFFERENT THAN MAN'S TIMING.

I (Tonilee) call this kind of occurrence an example of *God's near timing.* This prophecy and those from Isaiah 8:3 and 9:1-7 also referred to the coming of Jesus through Mary, which illustrates what I call *God's far timing.*

God's timing is completely different than man's timing, and of course that prophecy about the Messiah didn't come to pass until hundreds of years later. So know that as God gives you verses, the fulfillment of them may come in a near timing or a far timing. I've seen that with verses the Lord has given me concerning my children that keep unfolding in their lives over time because it's a continual process. God's timing is not your timing, but He has a near and a far timing, and He will work them both out on your behalf.

The next two truths go together:

4. God is always right, and 5. God always wins. When you face trouble or adversity, you can tell God you're angry, you can tell Him you're bitter, you can even tell Him you think He's wrong in the decisions He's making in your life. You may say to Him, "Lord, I don't understand where You are in this situation; I thought You were with me and the next thing I know, I feel like I am all alone," but the bottom line is, you must understand that He is God and you are not, and you need to submit to His authority. So after you let Him know how you feel, you need to say to Him, "Lord, Your will be done, not mine," and keep in mind that with the Lord's help, you can win this fight, even though it may take some time.

6. God's goal for you is that you keep your faith. First John 5:4 says, *...this is the victory that has overcome the world—our faith.* The victory isn't that the red carpet rolls out and we become queen or king for the day; the victory is that we keep our faith to the end. This verse tells us that the closer we walk with the Lord, the more issues are going to come into our life to develop our faith. The reason is that God is continually working with us to strengthen our faith and build our character to the point that nothing else matters to us but our faith.

Why is your faith so important? One time Jesus told Peter, *"Indeed, Satan has asked for you, that he may sift you as wheat. But I have prayed for you, that* **your faith should not fail***..."* (Luke 22:31-32, author's emphasis). It is by standing in faith (1 Corinthians 16:13) that we can win over every attack of the Enemy.

GOD IS CONTINUALLY WORKING WITH US TO STRENGTHEN OUR FAITH AND BUILD OUR CHARACTER.

7. God does everything through His love. Even if you are living in consequences from bad choices you've made, God has the ability to make it seem as if you were supposed to have done that wrong thing because He is able to turn your mistakes around and make them okay (Romans 8:28). You may find yourself looking back at your life from time to time saying, "Lord, I know I made a mistake, but oh, it's like roses now!" You may reach the place of not seeing the thorns anymore but just seeing the roses because God is able to make even your mistakes to prosper (Psalm 1:3).

God can work things together for good. He has that ability. But

GOD CAN WORK THINGS TOGETHER FOR GOOD. BUT DON'T LEAVE HIM; CONTINUE TO SEEK HIM EVERY DAY.

don't leave Him; continue to seek Him every day. If you leave Him, not only will you have to deal with the guilt that you left Him (even though He always remains faithful), but you're going to slow down the process of turning things around in your life. It's going to take longer to work through all that mess you made because the more mess you make, the more time it may take for the Lord to work it all together for good.

The goal is to stay with God so He can bless you quicker. He came and died for us so that we can receive life, and life in abundance (John 10:10). Our part is to stay with Him.

WAIT FOR THE PROMISE

When we start hearing God's voice in our hearts and He gives us a promise, we may not know what to do with it at first, and that's when we can run into a big problem. Abram (whose name was later changed to Abraham) is a perfect example. The Bible calls this man the father of our faith, yet he did something that we sometimes do too—he jumped to conclusions. We already saw how the Lord said to him:

> *"I will make you a great nation;*
> *I will bless you*
> *And make your name great;*
> *And you shall be a blessing.*
> *I will bless those who bless you,*

And I will curse him who curses you;
And in you all the families of the earth shall be blessed."
—Genesis 12:2-3

What you may not know is that when Abram departed from his homeland as the Lord had instructed, he was seventy-five years old, and he didn't have any children. Yet God had said that He was going to make Abram a nation, give him a name and blessing, and that every family on the earth was going to be blessed because of his family. Abram only had a wife and a nephew at that point, but he obeyed God and left home.

Eleven years of being obedient and faithful passed and Abram was still childless. Now he was eighty-six years old, but God came to him again and gave him the same promise. This time Abram said to the Lord, "You haven't given me an offspring yet, and my servant Eliezer is going to inherit everything" (15:2-3, author paraphrase), but God assured him, "*...this one shall not be your heir, but one who will come from your own body shall be your heir*" (Genesis 15:4).

At that point Abram must have been so excited at that word from the Lord. Can't you see him going home and saying to his wife, Sarai, "Isn't this great? I'm going to have a child, and it's going to come from my body. God clarified His promise and this child is going to come from me!"

Sarai was seventy-six years old then and she jumped to conclusions, probably thinking, "God didn't say it was going to come from my body, so maybe this is all about Abram. He wants a child so badly that he's convinced God told him that he's going to have a child." I believe that's how she felt because she came up with a plan to help God out.

Sarai said to Abram, "See now, the LORD has restrained me from bearing children. Please, go in to my maid; perhaps I shall obtain children by her." And Abram heeded the voice of Sarai.
—Genesis 16:2

Many Christians often jump to conclusions, as Sarai and Abram did, when they get a promise from God. We hear from God and think He means something He doesn't, and we forget that He has the absolute ability to independently make His promise happen in His way and in His time. He doesn't need us to do anything but believe. God cares more about your attitude toward Him so He can bless you His way, not with what your will wants. You may come to the Bible, wanting it to answer your circumstances like it's a crystal ball, but here's what often happens in that situation.

You may ask the Lord for something—maybe for a spouse—then you read a certain scripture that talks about God restoring a relationship and think it is saying that God is going to give you a special person in your life. Actually God might mean you and the Lord, not you and someone else. That's what Sarai (whose name was later changed to Sarah) did when she thought she knew how God wanted to give Abram a son. So she told Abram to go ahead and have a baby with her maid—and Ishmael was born.

GOD KEPT HIS PROMISE TO ABRAHAM EVEN THOUGH HE HAD JUMPED TO CONCLUSIONS— AND THE GRACE OF GOD WILL COVER OUR MISTAKES TOO.

Ishmael was not the son God had promised Abram, but having Ishmael did not negate the promise of God.

Twenty-five years later the Lord visited Sarah and did as he had spoken. Sarah conceived and bore Abraham a son in his old age at the set time of which God had spoken to him. Abraham called the name of his son, whom Sarah bore to him, Isaac and he circumcised Isaac when the child was eight days old, as God had commanded. (See Genesis 21:1-4.) God kept His promise to Abraham even though he had jumped to conclusions—and the grace of God will cover our mistakes too. If we do jump to conclusions and know we're wrong, it won't take away His promise to us.

The bottom line is, if God really gave you a promise, it will come to pass. You just have to believe and be obedient to His Word.

Abraham was one hundred years old when his son Isaac was born to him through Sarah. God gave him that promise and twenty-five years later, He fulfilled it. That may seem like a long time to wait, but sometimes God's promises can take a while to manifest in our lives today too. I'm sure you've heard about people who have been praying and praying for their spouse to fall in love with Jesus and at least come to church with them on Sunday mornings, and twenty-five years later it happened. Yet how many Christians don't want to wait for God's timing? Instead, they say, "Forget that, I'll just get a new spouse." Who wants to wait twenty-five years?

> IF GOD REALLY GAVE YOU A PROMISE, IT WILL COME TO PASS. YOU JUST HAVE TO BELIEVE AND BE OBEDIENT TO HIS WORD.

What they don't understand is that regardless of how long you have to wait for the promise to be fulfilled, you can start seeing the faithfulness of God in action in your life to carry you through. Not only does God want to bless you with the fulfillment of His promise to you, but He wants you to have the history of His faithfulness to you every year you had to depend on Him so you can see how He remained faithful to you through that time.

The Word of God has been a living testimony of His faithfulness to me time after time. I have memorial after memorial from circumstances that were so terrible that I can remember them vividly when I see the promises that God gave me to get me through them. When you are going through something that's hard and you see scriptures that God gave you that helped you get through hard times in the past, you are reminded that if God was faithful in all those other situations, this present circumstance will be a piece of cake for Him, and you will rest in the fact that He is going to give you the victory again.

CHOOSE TO SIT AT HIS FEET

One of the hardest questions for believers to answer is "How can you get to a point of hearing God talk to you regularly?" That's an amazing place to be—to be able to receive His wisdom wherever you go. In thinking back over the years that I've (Tonilee) been walking with the Lord, I remember growing and maturing to that point of being able to talk to the Lord all the time and to hear His voice in my heart no matter where I am. He often brings verses or other things back to my mind, and I understand what He is saying to me.

ASK THE LORD TO REVEAL HIS PLAN TO YOU. TALK TO THE LORD FIRST ABOUT ANY SITUATION YOU'RE FACING. WORSHIP.

I believe that you desire to hear God speak to you in that way or you would not be reading this book. Here are some steps I've learned that can help you.

The first step: Ask the Lord to reveal His plan to you. That comes from a verse I've always quoted in Amos 3:7 NIV that says, *Surely the...LORD does nothing without revealing his plan to his servants the prophets.* You can see that this first step is scriptural.

The second step: Talk to the Lord first about any situation you're facing. When incidences come into your life and you have to make choices, instead of reasoning it out with your best friend or with your spouse or picking up the phone and calling your mother, start talking to the Lord about it: "Lord, what about this," and "Lord, what about that," and "This is how much it's going to cost, but this is how much I make." Just talk to Him and start laying it all out. At this point you're not listening to Him, you're discussing it with Him before making any choice or decision. In other words, just talk to the Lord about it and include Him in your thought process.

The third step: Worship. Remember that in practicing the presence of worship, you come to the Lord in a place of quietness and stillness, and acknowledge who He is. Worship is a place of giving Him your whole heart and telling Him that you know He is so big that He can change any circumstance in your life, and letting Him know that you are going to submit to Him. In that place of worship, as God becomes bigger and bigger to you, it can become a time of repentance when you can begin to confess your sins and tell Him that you're so thankful for His grace and mercy.

When your heart is repentant, it will be humble, contrite, and broken, and you can open His Word and say, "I am not leaving until You talk to me about this situation." Then you can listen to what He has to tell you because you're in a place of listening, not talking anymore. You have said everything there was to say, and you're just going to listen. When you are in that place, God can reveal to you His plans, which might start with your rela-

THE ONLY WAY TO KNOW GOD'S WAYS IS TO SIT AT HIS FEET.

tionship with Him. When He reveals those plans, you can ask Him to confirm it in His Word.

This process may seem difficult at first, and you may feel at times like you don't want to do it, but think of it like this: It is your life. If you know Jesus is your Lord and Savior, you're going to spend eternity with Him so you might as well get to know His ways down here.

The only way to know God's ways is to sit at His feet.

Now it happened as they went that He [Jesus] entered a certain village; and a certain woman named Martha welcomed Him into her house. And she had a sister called Mary, who also sat at Jesus' feet and heard His word. But Martha was distracted with much serving, and she approached Him and said, "Lord, do You not care that my sister has left me to serve alone? Therefore tell her to help me." And Jesus answered and said to her, "Martha,

Martha, you are worried and troubled about many things. But one thing is needed, and Mary has chosen that good part, which will not be taken away from her."

—Luke 10:38-42

The worldly hindrances to hearing God's voice are pretty obvious; we can accept that we may watch too much television or that we get too busy with family or outside activities or that we are too distracted

WE CAN BE HINDERED FROM HEARING GOD'S VOICE JUST BY DOING THINGS FOR GOD.

with other forms of entertainment. But did you know that we can be hindered from hearing God's voice just by doing things for God? In this passage Martha had prepared her home for the Lord, yet Jesus rebuked her for serving Him.

If you've ever had a Bible fellowship in your home, you know how much effort can go into preparing for each meeting. Here we see Martha serving the Lord—Jesus was literally in her house. No doubt she'd spent much of the day preparing for His visit, and now when she needed help, her sister was in the living room with Him.

Can you imagine how we would be if Jesus was sitting in our living room? There probably wouldn't be a rug left in our house because we would have vacuumed so many times before He arrived, not to mention dusting the furniture, shining the silver, and preparing the food. We'd just be frantic.

Our hearts would be in the right place, as Martha's was, because we would just want to serve the Lord. Yet Jesus told Martha, "You're missing it." The problem was that Martha was busy being hospitable and tending to the Lord's natural needs (like food), but she stayed so busy serving the Lord that she ignored her own spiritual needs. Now doing the Lord's work is important but not to the point that you lose your focus on a relationship with Him.

On the other hand, Mary was spending time in Jesus' presence, sitting at His feet, listening to His Word—*logos*, the divine Word of God, the same Word we read about in John 1:14 (the Word is Jesus). When this passage says that Mary sat at Jesus' feet, it means that she was "a disciple" of His, that she listened attentively to His instructions and was anxious to learn His doctrine—His Word.[1]

Here in Martha's living room Jesus was speaking the Word of God to those who were listening, and He told Martha that Mary had chosen to do the better thing because Mary was tending to her spiritual needs. She was getting to know His will and His ways. You see, we have a choice—both are commendable, but "sitting at Jesus' feet" is the best.

WE HAVE TO CHOOSE TO "SIT AT HIS FEET" FIRST.

We can be busy doing all kinds of activities to please the Lord and yet those can be the very things that distract us from reading His Word and hearing His voice (which is how we get to know His ways). So we have to choose to "sit at His feet" first.

If you think that you have wasted your life by making the wrong choice, Bobbye has some good news.

RESTORING THE LOCUST YEARS

I (Bobbye) was in my mid-thirties when I realized that God had changed my life for a different purpose than what I could have ever imagined, and I found myself so remorseful that I had wasted so much time. I remember saying to the Lord, "Why didn't I know this? Why didn't I do this right after I left college? I could have been serving You for at least the last twenty years," and the Lord led me to the second chapter of Joel (remember, this is one way the Holy Spirit speaks to us). I was reading along one day when I came down to verse 25.

*"I will restore to you the years
that the swarming locust has eaten,
The crawling locust,
The consuming locust,
And the chewing locust,
My great army which I sent among you.
You shall eat in plenty and be satisfied,
And praise the name of the LORD your God.*
—Joel 2:25-26

Those words really jumped out at me in the depths of my heart, and I heard God say to me, "It's okay, Bobbye, I'll restore the years of the locust. I'll restore all those years that you could have been doing what I planned for you to do." See, I still had a choice to sit at His feet or just be busy doing my own thing, but this promise He gave me says that it doesn't matter that I made the wrong choice for years because He can restore them back to me—and this promise from His Word is the same for you as it is for me.

GOD DOESN'T KEEP A CHRONOLOGICAL CLOCK LIKE WE DO OR LOOK AT THINGS THE WAY WE DO.

My heart just leaped because it was such an impression in me that I serve an awesome God who has the kind of power to do that in our lives. It's not physically, humanly possible to have those years restored and to find yourself at a place of doing things that are beyond you. Yet as I began to read the Bible, in a very short period of time my knowledge of the Word began to grow and along with it came wisdom. Soon things that were not possible for me to do in the natural began to happen because it was the power of God working in my life, and it was as though I'd always known this Word.

God doesn't keep a chronological clock like we do or look at things the way we do. For instance, you get your high school diploma in twelve years, then your bachelor's degree in four years, and your master's degree in two. He can turn your life around in a moment and get you on the right path and make it seem as if you have always been living this way. All it takes is being truly willing to seek His presence, listen to His voice, and hear what He has to say to you.

[GOD] CAN TURN YOUR LIFE AROUND IN A MOMENT AND GET YOU ON THE RIGHT PATH AND MAKE IT SEEM AS IF YOU HAVE ALWAYS BEEN LIVING THIS WAY.

We pray that if nothing else, you will finish reading this book with a new understanding of what it means to practice God's presence and with a different and even greater appreciation for His Word. It is the air we breathe, it is the bread we eat through His Holy Spirit, and through it we have access to knowing everything He wants us to know. There are certain mysteries and revelations we all will not be privy to until we get to heaven, but Bobbye and I believe with all our hearts that it is His will for you to know absolutely much more than you can even imagine or think on your own.

The moment you make the commitment to be in God's presence every day, to let Him be in charge of every decision you are going to make, to ask Him what He wants you to do even if it goes against what you think is right or what you think you should be doing, you're connected to your heavenly Father, and there is no better place to be. Yet so many believers have never experienced that kind of extraordinary relationship.

Living without being connected to God is similar to the old cell phone I (Tonilee) recently gave my eight-year-old daughter (at the time this book is being written). I got a new cell phone so I gave my old one to her, and she just loves to play with it. That old cell phone has no connection, but she still plugs it in and charges it. Sometimes she puts it in her pocket and carries it around and charges it in the car and pretends people are calling her because she plays with the ringer. She doesn't care that the cell phone is not connected; she's perfectly content to play with a dead cell phone.

How many Christians are like that when it comes to the Lord?

THESE DAYS ARE SHORT AND TO BE IN THE PRESENCE OF GOD, DESPITE ALL THE HORRORS OF THE WORLD, NEEDS TO BE OUR TOP PRIORITY.

They love to play church or to play Christianity, but they are not connected to Him, so they have no power in their lives, no peace or joy or guidance, no two-way communication with Him, and no real answers to their troubles. When you have a cell phone company connect your cell phone, you have a whole new world in front of you. A whole new world awaits those who connect to God by practicing His presence.

There's nothing else like it because your perspective will change from this temporal life here to the eternal. Nothing else will matter to you except those you love and those in this world that you know need Jesus. All of a sudden you will become aware of other people who need what you have with God. You will even realize that some people who are born again need to know more about how to live in the Lord's presence. So your heart's desire will be to do everything you can to spread that message and to bring them in because this life is quickly passing away.

These days are short and to be in the presence of God, despite all the horrors of the world, needs to be our top priority. Pick up the newspaper, turn on the news—it's not going to get any better, ever. That's a biblical fact. (See Matthew 24.) But God always has the answers we need, and they can be found in His presence.

When the Israelites forsook the Lord's ways, stopped worshiping Him, and stopped communicating with Him, they turned to the world's ways and ended up in destructive habits. But when they practiced God's ways of worship and kept all of His commands for them, they were blessed because they lived under His protection.

If you have begun to practice worship, prayer, and hearing His voice, not only will you be blessed and protected, but the desires of your heart will lead you to a place of living for Christ. It is not just a matter of worship, prayer, or reading the Word at certain times, but it is the whole package that must comprise your daily life.

Our prayer for you is that this book has jump-started you and given you the desire and the tools to seek God, beginning today. It starts with a commitment in your heart and mind to go forth and pursue His presence, but the blessings you will experience will be extraordinary—a life of grace, power, and abundance.

BUILDING BLOCKS
■■■■■■■■■■

- Question 1: From 2 Chronicles 16:7-9, answer these questions.
  a. What did King Asa do that caused him to lose the war?

  b. Think of a difficulty you've been through recently. Did you still seek the Lord or did it cause you to turn away from Him? Explain.

■ Questions 2: Read 1 Samuel 30 to answer these questions.
   a. How did David encourage himself in the Lord and recover all that the enemy had stolen from him?

   b. Write down the seven ways to encourage yourself in the Lord and how you can implement them in your life.

■ Question 3: Read Genesis 16.
   a. How did Abraham and Sarah jump to conclusions about what God had told them? What were the results?

   b. Have you ever jumped to conclusions when you received a word from the Lord? Why or why not?

■ Question 4: What are the three steps to hearing God's voice?

■ Questions 5: Read Luke 10:38-42 to answer the following questions.
   a. When Jesus was visiting Mary and Martha's home, why was Mary doing the better thing?

   b. Describe in your own words what it means to sit at the feet of Jesus. When was the last time you did that yourself? Explain.

■ Question 6: Read Joel 2:24-26 to answer these questions.
  a. How has God changed your life?

  b. Do you feel as if you've wasted much of your life going in the wrong direction? How does Joel 2:24-26 encourage you?

  c. Do you believe that God can restore your locust years? Why or why not?

ENDNOTES

CHAPTER 1

1. Brown, Driver, Briggs and Gesenius, *The KJV Old Testament Hebrew Lexicon*, "Hebrew Lexicon entry for Paniym," available from http://www.biblestudytools.net/Lexicons/Hebrew/heb.cgi?number=6440&version=kjv, S.V. "presence," Exodus 33:14.

2. Based on information from Albert Barnes, *Barnes' Notes on the Bible*, available from http://www.e-sword.net/commentaries.html, S.V. "John 15:15."

3. Matthew Henry, *Matthew Henry Complete Commentary on the Whole Bible*, "Commentary on Exodus 33," available from http://bible.crosswalk.com/Commentaries/MatthewHenryComplete/mhc-com.cgi?book=ex&chapter=033, S.V. "Exodus 33:7-11."

4. Ibid., S.V. "Exodus 33:1-6."

5. Ibid.

CHAPTER 3

1. Albert Barnes, S.V. "Will manifest myself to him," John 14:21.

2. *Robertson's Word Pictures in the New Testament*, available from http://www.e-sword.net/commentaries.html, S.V. "And will manifest myself to him," John14:21.

3. Thayer and Smith, *The KJV New Testament Greek Lexicon*, "Greek Lexicon entry for Meno," available from http://www.bible studytools.net/Lexicons/Greek/grk.cgi?number=3306&version=kjv, S.V. "abide," John 15:7.

CHAPTER 4

1. The Passover is a Jewish feast that celebrates how the angel of death passed over the people who had painted the blood of a lamb on their doorposts, according to God's instructions to Moses, and spared the lives of their firstborn.

CHAPTER 5

1. Based on information from *Keil and Delitzsch Commentary on the Old Testament*, available from http://www.e-sword.net/commentaries.html, S.V. "Genesis 4:2-7."

2. Adam Clarke, *Adam Clarke Commentary of the Whole Bible*, available from http://www.e-sword.net/commentaries.html, S.V. "God is a Spirit," John 4:24.

3. *Merriam-Webster's Collegiate Dictionary*, 11th ed. (Springfield, Massachusetts: Merriam-Webster, Inc., 2003), S.V. "sanctify."

4. Thayer and Smith, "Greek Lexicon entry for Hagiazo," available from http://www.biblestudytools.net/Lexicons/Greek/grk.cgi?number=37&version=kjv, S.V. "sanctify," John 17:17.

5. Jesus' blood cleanses us from our sins. (1 John 1:7). We become covered in His blood when we become born again, and we can also "plead" His blood over ourselves and others by speaking that out loud.

6. Thayer and Smith, "Greek Lexicon entry for Latreuo," available from http://www.biblestudytools.net/Lexicons/Greek/grk.cgi?number=3000&version=kjv, S.V. "worship."

CHAPTER 6

1. Thayer and Smith, "Greek Lexicon entry for Nike," available from http://www.biblestudytools.net/Lexicons/Greek/grk.cgi?number=3529&version=kjv, S.V. "victory," 1 John 5:4.

2. Albert Barnes, S.V. "veil," Matthew 27:51.

3. Based on a definition from Merriam-Webster, S.V. "power of attorney."

CHAPTER 7

1. Adam Clarke, S.V. "Genesis 6:8."

2. Merriam-Webster, S.V. "grace."

3. Brown, Driver, Briggs and Gesenius, "Hebrew Lexicon entry for Chen," available from http://www.biblestudytools.net/Lexicons/Hebrew/heb.cgi?number=2580&version=kjv, s.v. "grace," Genesis 6:8.

4. Thayer and Smith, "Greek Lexicon entry for Charis," available from http://www.biblestudytools.net/Lexicons/Greek/grk.cgi?number=5485&version=kjv, S.V. "grace."

5. Walter A. Elwell, *Evangelical Dictionary of Theology*, "Entry for 'Theophany,'" available from http://bible.crosswalk.com/Dictionaries/BakersEvangelicalDictionary/bed.cgi?number=T690.

6. Based on a definition from Brown, Driver, Briggs and Gesenius, "Hebrew Lexicon entry for Natah," available from http://www.biblestudytools.net/Lexicons/Hebrew/heb.cgi?number=5186&version=kjv, S.V. "incline," John 10:27.

7. Thayer and Smith, "Greek Lexicon entry for Logos," available from http://www.biblestudytools.net/Lexicons/Greek/grk.cgi?number=3056&version=kjv, s.v. "word," John 1:14.

CHAPTER 8

1. Based on information from Albert Barnes, s.v. "sat at Jesus' feet," Luke 10:39.

ABOUT THE AUTHORS

BOBBYE BROOKS AND TONILEE ADAMSON MET AT a church Bible study in 2000 in San Diego, California. They became fast friends as well as committed prayer partners. They soon discovered a shared passion and desire to teach others how to have a daily walk with Jesus Christ by studying the Bible and learning how to pray. They co-founded *Daily Disciples Ministries* in 2002 with a heart to evangelize the lost and awaken the saved by teaching, training, and encouraging everyone to apply the Bible to their daily lives. Bobbye and Tonilee hold conferences, teach Bible studies, and conduct discipleship training programs to carry out the mission of Daily Disciples, as they desire for all to become a daily disciple of Jesus Christ.

Their radio program, "Daily Disciples Radio," is a daily thirty-minute teaching program that airs on stations throughout the country. The program includes teaching and in-studio discussions on how to apply the Word of God to everyday life.

Bobbye and her husband, Tom, make their home in Carlsbad, California. Tonilee and her husband, Rob, are the parents of three children and live in San Diego, California.